Policin

College

Policing and Criminology

Policing Matters

Policing and Criminology

Craig Paterson
Ed Pollock

Series editors
P A J Waddington
Martin Wright

LearningMatters

First published in 2011 by Learning Matters Ltd

British Library Cataloguing in Publication Data
A CIP record for this book is available from the British Library.

ISBN: 978 0 85725 413 9

This book is also available in the following ebook formats:

Adobe ebook   ISBN: 978 0 85725 415 3
EPUB ebook   ISBN: 978 0 85725 414 6
Kindle   ISBN: 978 0 85725 416 0

Cover and text design by Toucan Design
Project Management Newgen Publishing and Data Services
Typeset by Newgen Publishing and Data Services
Printed and bound in Great Britain by Short Run Press Ltd, Exeter, Devon

Learning Matters Ltd
20 Cathedral Yard
Exeter EX1 1HB
Tel: 01392 215560
info@learningmatters.co.uk
www.learningmatters.co.uk

All weblinks and web addresses in this book have been carefully checked prior to publication, but for up-to-date information please visit the Learning Matters website, www.learningmatters.co.uk.

Contents

1 An introduction to criminology

CHAPTER OBJECTIVES

By the end of this chapter you should be able to:

- identify the historical links between policing and criminological study;
- identify essential criminological tools and their role in researching the police and policing;
- identify different criminological theories;
- understand the role of criminological study in researching the police and policing.

LINKS TO STANDARDS

This chapter provides opportunities for links with the following Skills for Justice, National Occupational Standards (NOS) for Policing and Law Enforcement 2008.

AE1   Maintain and develop your own knowledge, skills and competence.
CA1   Use law enforcement actions in a fair and justified way.
HA2   Manage your own resources and professional development.

Introduction

Policing has been a subject of social inquiry throughout the history of the United Kingdom (from now onwards the UK), across Europe, and further afield. From the Knights Templar in the Holy Land during the Crusades to the Spanish Inquisition in early modern Europe, history provides us with numerous examples of famous (and infamous) groups and individuals whose job it was to police social order. The study of policing, therefore, pre-dates criminology and criminologists by centuries. In contemporary societies, the Police Service, as an institution, and policing, as a key social function, are key components of democratic social order across the world. This societal position makes careful scrutiny of the role and function of the Police Service essential, and criminologists have taken it upon themselves to develop numerous critiques of the ways in which the police and policing operate within societies.

This book provides an introduction to the criminological study of policing which, in the Anglo-American context, emerged during the 1960s and has remained a core constituent of criminological study ever since. Over the past decade, a new academic area of study has come to the fore, police studies, which draws on criminological study and other academic subjects. The following pages will provide you with a guide to the broad contours of police studies and criminology plus the contribution each can make to understanding developments in policing in the UK and elsewhere.

Criminological inquiry revolves around two central areas.

1. Analysis of the causes of crime.

2. Evaluation and analysis of methods of crime control.

This twin focus on why people commit crime and how societies manage crime problems provides the bedrock of the academic discipline of criminology. Criminological study of the police emerged out of the social conflict of the 1960s, which bore witness to an acceleration in social change that was accompanied by urban unrest, political protest and new social problems for the police to manage. Early studies identified a perception of the police's role as crime fighters, both within the police and from outside, while empirical studies (the cornerstone of criminological inquiry) provided evidence of the police's role in maintaining social order and keeping the peace. It is important to note at this stage that the focus of this book is policing and criminology in the UK. Policing in the UK is split into three jurisdictions: England and Wales, Scotland, and Northern Ireland, although there are a number of national agencies that operate across all three areas. Although consideration is given of policing institutions and processes across the world (particularly in Chapter 8), this is mainly used to provide analytical context which helps us understand developments in the UK.

PRACTICAL TASK

Before you read on any further, have a think about what the main crime problems are in your area. Now have a look at your local crime and policing website (www. police.uk/). Are the crime problems that the statistics highlight the same as the ones you imagined?

The purpose of the book

The book highlights the links between the academic discipline of criminology, developments in policing and the police profession to bridge the gap between academic study and police practice. In order to do this, the book examines the development of the Police Service and their changing role in society. Links are made between criminological theory and police responses to offending and disorder, and the reader is introduced to a range of policing theories, the role of values and ethics and the multi-agency context of twenty-first century policing. The book provides an introduction to criminological perspectives on the development of the Police Service in England and Wales over the past 200 years alongside an overview of key contemporary themes in policing. Key topics include the changing role of policing in society, police governance and accountability, policing philosophies and strategies, the pluralisation of policing and the globalisation of policing. The book also examines the role criminology has played in the police reform and modernisation agenda and the shift to evidence-led approaches to policing. It also provides key information and learning materials for students on criminology and policing courses.

The structure of the book

This chapter introduces readers to the academic subject of criminology and its relationship with policing. A brief history of policing research is provided, and this is followed by an overview of links between criminological theories and developments in policing functions. Chapter 2 outlines the circumstances in which the 'new police' were established in England and Wales during the nineteenth century and provides an introduction to criminological accounts of the historical development of the police. Chapter 3 discusses the changing role and function of the Police Service throughout the twentieth century. A historical account of dominant policing philosophies and strategies is provided along with links to changing criminological perspectives on offending. Chapter 4 looks specifically at the contribution criminology has made to the study of policing during the second half of the twentieth century and the development of police studies over the past decade. Links will be made to the 'crisis of legitimacy' that the police experienced during the 1970s and 1980s in order to provide context for the later chapters on police reform.

Chapter 5 introduces readers to the re-invention of community policing during a historical period when consent towards the police from communities could no longer be guaranteed. Chapter 6 develops focus on police reform and looks at the pluralisation of policing provision and the impact this has had on the role of the Police Service and other agencies. Chapter 7 focuses on contemporary debates about police ethics and police reform in addition to presenting key arguments in previous chapters in an ethical or value-based context. Chapter 8 introduces students to the connections between the globalisation of crime and policing responses to crime. This includes the impact on policing of new technologies, global trade, population mobility and human trafficking, serious and organised crime, terrorism and other important contemporary topics. Finally, Chapter 9 discusses the likely shape of policing in the UK as we move further into the twenty-first century. In particular, the chapter considers how the Police Service might be required to contribute to multi-agency initiatives alongside other policing and offender management agencies, as well as with the contemporary focus on active citizens.

What do you think are the main responsibilities and duties of the Police Service in the UK? The Home Office's Police Service website (www.homeoffice.gov.uk/ police/) provides you with an introduction to the many and varied responsibilities of the twenty-first century police.

Researching the police

Although criminological research of the police did not begin until the 1960s, there is an extensive range of sources of historical data which allows us to research the role that the Police Service has played in society since its establishment in 1829. Early histories of the police portray the creation of the police institution as part of the enlightenment progress towards a more civilised society and a legacy of benevolent police reformers with great foresight. This perspective was challenged from the 1970s onwards as critics of the police challenged this consensus vision of the police role. Despite this sustained critique, the criminological importance of the early histories lay in identifying the policy process through which the police institution was established as a key source of criminological analysis. This focus on contemporary public and private debates in addition to policy document analysis remain a part of the process of understanding governmental aims today and is a core constituent of all of the three main areas of police research.

- Sociological analysis of the police and policing.

- Cultural analysis of the police institution.

- Critiques of the police role and function, philosophies and strategies.

The sociological perspective

Until the 1950s the police were not subjected to in-depth social scientific study. This changed with the publication of Michael Banton's (1964) *The Policeman in the Community*. Banton challenged the dominant policing narrative, which had been created by former senior police officers, civil servants and politicians, and which made links between the police and social stability and order. Banton's work paved the way for a multitude of sociological studies of the police that shone a new light on the police role and emphasised the importance of peace-keeping ahead of crime fighting.

Banton was conducting his research at a time (1960–63) when public allegations of police corruption and misconduct were becoming increasingly prevalent. Banton's research was published at the same time as the introduction of the 1964 Police Act that reformed the structure of the Police Service in England and Wales in response to concerns about police inefficiency and impropriety and this made him the first criminologist to recognise the importance of the role of the police officer in society (police–community relations) and the use (and misuse) of police discretion, though his analysis was framed by a consensual vision of society. The most prominent contemporary development in the social scientific study of the police has been in an area known as administrative criminology. Administrative criminology is normally funded by central government or individual police forces and uses specific research methodologies to evaluate the efficiency and effectiveness of different police, as well as other criminal justice, initiatives.

The cultural perspective

The police are a cultural institution that symbolise certain aspects of Britishness in the same way as the Anglican Church, the British monarchy, and fish and chips. Following on from Banton, many criminologists in the UK looked specifically at the role of police culture and the administration of street-level justice by police officers. Using mainly ethnographic methodologies, where a researcher submerges himself or herself in the occupational culture of an organisation, a body of literature on British police culture was built up by scholars such as Reiner (2010), Holdaway (1984) and Fielding (1988) throughout the late 1970s and 1980s. This literature highlighted the importance of 'cop culture' to policing as a consequence of the discretion that police officers are allowed when undertaking everyday police work.

Street-level policing often takes place away from the eyes of sergeants and inspectors and is subsequently rendered invisible from managerial figures. At first, the 'cop culture' literature focused upon the role of 'street cops' rather than managers and because of this it was often referred to as 'canteen culture'. Much of the early literature on cop culture highlighted the negative impact of the culture upon operational policing, particularly where the police did not provide a fair and equitable service to the public and discriminated according to age, ethnicity, gender, religion, sexuality or class. Since the 1990s, academic work on police culture has provided a more balanced and nuanced appreciation of the operational impact of the occupational culture on street-level policing (Chan, 1996; Waddington, 1999), although the ethnographic methods of early researchers are used more sparingly due to the high costs of this methodological approach and the lack of control it provides over errant researchers!

The conflict perspective

During the 1970s and 1980s the police experienced a 'crisis of legitimacy' as public trust in the institution waned and crime rates increased. The relationship between the police and minority ethnic groups illuminated a growing mistrust and malaise among the general public regarding the role of the state in civil society. The period 1980–85 bore witness to sustained civil unrest and sporadic outbreaks of urban disorder that highlighted the changing relationship between an increasingly diverse society and unreformed police forces. The civil disturbances of this period initiated a renewed focus upon the police's use of their power, discretion and status and produced a body of criminological literature that challenged the consensus perspective of a police 'thin blue line' that protected society from crime and disorder.

Challenging the actions of the police is an essential function of democratic societies as this helps maintain the quality of the relationship between the police and civic society. The provision of effective and equitable policing services (or the perception thereof) is a precondition of a democratic political structure as policing in democratic societies takes place within a political landscape that acknowledges the importance of social justice, social cohesion, fairness, equity and human rights. The requirements of democratic policing emphasise the importance of police professionalism, accountability and legitimacy. There is a clear link between the professional use of discretion, understood as making appropriate situational judgements, and the broader issues of public accountability and police legitimacy. This makes academic analysis of the police role from all three perspectives an essential component of the function of criminology. The impact of this work has been evident in the strategic shift to service-oriented, community policing in response to the 'crisis of police legitimacy'.

REFLECTIVE TASK

Which of these criminological research traditions do you think benefits wider society the most? The answer you provide to this question will provide some clues to the criminological theories and perspectives that you will favour throughout your studies.

A number of recurring yet different criminological theories can be identified in each of the research traditions identified above, most obviously those that fit into the broad consensus and conflict perspectives. The rest of this chapter provides an overview of the most relevant criminological theories and identifies the particular historical periods when these theories influenced policing or perspectives on policing, as well as their enduring impact on policing policy. The main objective of a criminological theory is to provide an explanation of offending behaviour and, in some cases, criminal justice responses to offending behaviour. The following section also refers to criminological perspectives which incorporate several, often interconnected criminological theories rather than several often similar, criminological theories. It is important to recognise that no single criminological theory provides an overarching explanation of crime and policing responses to it but that, as criminologists, we are required to use a mixture of different theories to explain why people offend and to design methods and strategies to reduce offending behaviour and the harm that it causes to society.

Policing and criminological theory

In *The New Policing* (2007, page 49) Eugene McLaughlin points to four theoretical perspectives that have dominated police studies and criminological analysis of the police institution since the 1960s: symbolic interactionist, Marxist, administrative, Left Realist. In this section, we extend McLaughlin's categories to include several additional theoretical perspectives that have influenced the evolution of the police institution throughout its near 200-year history. We will revisit these theoretical perspectives throughout the book to help the reader make links between developments in policing and the changing role and influence of criminological scholarship throughout its 50-year history.

Each of the following sections provides a short introduction to the core concepts and key thinkers associated with a criminological theory. Make a note of your interpretation of each of these theories and use the notes to identify the different theoretical perspectives that appear throughout this book.

The classical school

In Chapter 2, the reader is introduced to two of the key intellectual figures who influenced the establishment of the 'new police' – Henry Fielding (1707–54) and Patrick Colquhoun (1745–1820). Both Fielding and Colquhoun perceived the role of the police to be the provision of an 'unremitting gaze' over disorderly areas and populations. From their perspective, the presence of the police officer was intended to invoke self-discipline in deviant individuals and assist in the restoration of social order through the general deterrence of a potentially problematic urban population. The idea of the unremitting gaze was taken from Jeremy Bentham (1748–1832), a philosopher and social reformer, who looked at ways in which the governing structures of society could mould the free will of individuals to encourage them to act in a more pro-social way.

Like Cesare Beccaria (1738–94), Bentham saw 'the greatest happiness for the greatest number' as the utilitarian aim of all public policy, and alongside other enlightenment thinkers, Bentham and Beccaria came to be seen as the founders of the classical school of criminology. Classical thought was underpinned by a view that people are rational creatures who seek pleasure and avoid pain. Therefore, this instinct could be moulded through societal governance to create human beings who are happy to comply with the law and society's wider interests. The aim of the law and the role of the police were simply to protect society from harm. Modern theories of social control (Foucault, 1977, Cohen, 1985, Garland, 1996) cite the classical perspective of regulating and disciplining the behaviour of individuals in explaining the growth of CCTV, speed cameras and other forms of surveillance which aim to guide our behaviour through general deterrence. The classical perspective also provides the foundations of rational choice theory and routine activities theory that underpin administrative criminology.

Durkheim and 'anomie'

Emile Durkheim (1858–1917) developed the first fully sociological explanation of crime, and his ideas inspired a generation of sociologists of juvenile delinquency in the United States (hereafter US) known as the Chicago School. The Chicago School subsequently shifted criminological explanations away from a focus on the psychological theories of Sigmund Freud (1856–1939) and the biological theories of Cesare Lombroso (1835–1909) and towards sociological explanations of crime. Although Durkheim's core concepts of 'anomie', a 'collective conscience' and 'mechanical solidarity' first came to the fore in the late nineteenth century they continue to be of relevance to policing today. According to popular memory, the 1950s and 1960s were characterised by high levels of community cohesion and policing that was underpinned by community (or 'mechanical solidarity'; see Durkheim, 1933, page 226) solidarity unlike the present era when consent towards the police from communities has become increasingly contested.

Using Durkheim's theoretical perspective, the relationship between policing and society can be understood through analysis of social change. Thus, the police institution was established during a period of social and political unrest in the early to mid-nineteenth century, and subsequent policing crises have similarly occurred at times of rapid social change and conflict. These include the mid-1960s when conflict perspectives became established in criminology and a new policing settlement was agreed in the form of the 1964 Police Act (see Chapter 3); the 'crisis of legitimacy' in the 1970s which was characterised by conflict between minority groups and the police (see Chapter 5) and rising fear of crime from the 1990s onwards that has accompanied the rapid processes of globalisation (see Chapter 8). Rapid social change can provide challenges for the notion of policing by consent that underpins policing in the UK and has current policy relevance because of the Liberal–Conservative emphasis placed upon a Big Society (of mechanical solidarity) of active citizens who are expected to assume a more significant policing and surveillance role than before.

Social disorganisation

The Chicago School of Sociology developed Durkheim's ideas and created an understanding of crime as an often intentioned response to prevailing social conditions. Robert Park placed 'human ecology' at the centre of this analysis (a concept that would later evolve into the field of environmental criminology) where social disorganisation, or the relationship between people and the character of the territory they inhabited, influenced crime rates. In their book *The City*, Park and Ernest Burgess (1925) developed this concept further and pointed towards the high levels of crime and deviance in geographical areas with transient populations and an absence of social integration. The most vulnerable area became known as the 'zone of transition' and was characterised by high rates of immigration, infant mortality, mental disorder, truancy and welfare subsistence (Shaw and McKay, 1942). Because of this, economically successful individuals and families moved out of this area as soon as this was possible, a process that led to the area being characterised by high, and entrenched, levels of social deprivation.

The Chicago School's sociological positivism (the idea that the social environment influences individual and group behaviour) retained an influence over criminology and public policy until the latter part of the twentieth century and still helps our understanding of crime patterns in urban areas. Despite this, the large-scale entrance of government into the housing market in the UK during the 1960s dramatically altered the human ecology of cities, and this process was accentuated by the 1980s 'right to buy' local authority housing initiative which further intensified levels of deprivation in some urban areas. The regeneration of UK cities from the 1990s onwards was driven, in part, by recognition of the links between crime, disorder and the environment. From a policing perspective, this raises the question of how high levels of crime in urban areas can be controlled. Environmental criminology has driven a twin focus on the identification of crime 'hotspots' through empirical measurement and designing-out crime from urban areas. The focus on crime prevention from the 1980s onwards was driven by a belief that the urban environment could be re-designed to discourage criminality and this led to the growth in urban crime prevention techniques such as enhanced surveillance through CCTV and improved street lighting in at-risk areas. In addition to this, most police forces now employ crime analysts who identify concentrations of specific types of criminality to inform intelligence-led or problem-oriented policing responses to these crime problems.

REFLECTIVE TASK

Is it possible to identify a 'zone of transition' in the area that you live in? The twenty-first century city is much more complex than Chicago in the 1920s. To what extent do you think that the concepts of 'human ecology' and 'social disorganisation' have relevance to urban life today?

Strain and sub-culture

In the 1930s, Robert Merton, inspired by writers from the Chicago School of Sociology, adapted Durkheim's concept of 'anomie' and applied it to America's experience of the Great Depression. Merton defined 'anomie', or strain as he referred to it, as a breakdown in the social structure that took place when a disjunction appeared between cultural norms and goals and the socially structured capacities of individuals to respond successfully to them. According to Merton, in the US, society was geared and people were socialised towards the shared goals of 'the American dream'; however, the goal of the American dream was not equally obtainable by everyone. The failure of the American dream produced a strain within society which, in some cases, produced a deviant response such as offending behaviour (Merton, 1938, page 672). Merton's concept of 'strain' subsequently inspired a multitude of sub-cultural theorists who used his ideas to explain the prevalence of delinquent behaviour among young males in post–Second World War American society (see Cohen, 1955, and Matza, 1964, for two prominent examples). In the mid-1960s, sub-cultural theory began to have an impact on criminology in the UK (see Downes, 1966) and continues to have an influence on cultural criminology which focuses on an understanding of the attraction, meaning and interpretation of deviant behaviour (Ferrell et al., 2008).

REFLECTIVE TASK

Sub-cultural theorists focus mainly on the deviant and offending behaviour of young males. Why do you think that young males commit such a high proportion of recorded criminal offences?

Labelling

Labelling (or symbolic interactionist) theorists view the emphasis placed on social structure by many sub-cultural theorists as overly simplistic and, instead, encourage a greater focus on class conflict and the creativity of youthful rebellion against existing social structures. Labelling perspectives shift the lens of analysis towards the role of the criminal justice system in constructing criminal behaviour and the different ways in which individuals respond to the deviant label (Lemert, 1951). From a policing perspective this raises questions about the discriminatory use of police discretion and the process through which deviant behaviour becomes criminalised as offenders interact with the label that has been placed upon them by the police. Labelling perspectives point towards the crucial role played by the police as gatekeepers to the criminal justice system and the necessity of empirical studies to shed light on the low visibility of police work.

The most common methodological approach used by both sub-cultural and labelling theorists is ethnography. Ethnographers take a 'naturalistic' approach to research and attempt to embed themselves in the 'real world' environment of offenders and criminal justice practitioners. In many ways, criminological ethnographers have developed the work of Banton into the contemporary study of police culture with its emphasis on interpreting operational police work at the street level. The main critique of these approaches is that although they provide valuable intellectual insight into the working practices of police officers, ethnographers do not focus sufficiently upon policy implementation and contribute little to debates about how policing could be improved. The absence of a policy focus in ethnography has contributed to this methodological approach being displaced by administrative criminology from the early 1990s onwards with its more easily measurable focus upon statistical data and the efficiency of policing provision. The development of conflict perspectives such as labelling laid the ground for the influence of Marxism over criminological thought throughout the 1970s.

REFLECTIVE TASK

What sort of 'labels' do we ascribe to offenders? Have a quick think about various types of offending behaviour. What are the images that immediately come to mind? Be honest!

Marxism

Although it is widely acknowledged that Karl Marx (1818–83) had little to say about crime and criminal behaviour, Marxist scholars point towards the importance of structural inequality and deficits of power in interpreting crime and, more importantly, the responses of criminal justice agencies towards deviance and transgression. Marxist scholars, as well as other conflict theorists such as those who emerged out of the Birmingham School in the 1970s (see Chapter 5), encourage a greater criminological focus on the use and misuse of police authority as well as the injustices perpetrated by a self-serving 'police–state–class' relationship. Marxist theorists argue that in plural societies containing a multitude of groups with conflicting demands and values, an inevitable conflict ensues over limited power and resources. In unequal capitalist societies the powerful assert their strength through legislation that criminalises the behaviour of the powerless. Marxist writers challenge the existence of the principle of policing by consent and have instead constructed a critique of the police function that emphasises the police's role in maintaining social and political order while exacerbating social, cultural and sexual inequality.

Marxist perspectives provide a platform for the development of other conflict perspectives related to ethnicity, gender, sexuality and disability which place issues of (often state) power at the heart of criminological analysis. Marxist scholars encourage analysis of the impact of policing on minority ethnic groups as well as the hegemony of a masculine culture that subordinates the role of women (see Chapter 4). Marxist perspectives came to the fore at a time when senior police officers were becoming an increasingly prominent (and often authoritarian) public voice and questioned the extent to which the separation of the police from the political system, as set up in the 1964 Police Act, had been maintained. Similarly, the influence of Marxist feminists sought to explain the absence of the policing of sexual offences and domestic violence as well as the over-emphasis within criminology during the 1970s on male offenders compared to female victims.

REFLECTIVE TASK

Why are policing strategies focused on the behaviour of poor people living in deprived areas and not on the behaviour of those living in more affluent parts of the country?

The New Right

While Marxist criminological theories provided critical accounts about developments in modes of crime control during the 1970s, a multitude of right wing theories emerged at the same time that would have a much greater influence over developments in policing over the next three decades. The ideas of Classical School theorists were revived during the 1970s and 1980s as the idea of free-willed, rational thinking actors returned to the fore in criminology. In the UK the Home Office began to look at pro-active forms of crime prevention that would displace the previous emphasis upon offender motivation. This administrative approach viewed criminal behaviour as 'normal' (Garland, 1996), a problem to be managed, and set about combating rising levels of crime through methods that focused upon decreasing the likelihood of a crime taking place.

Administrative criminology

Administrative criminologists and rational choice theorists view crime as being driven by opportunity. From this perspective, motivation is a secondary or background factor. Cohen and Felson's (1979) routine activity approach encourages a triangular understanding of crime causation where the three factors that lead to a criminal act taking place are as follows.

- A motivated offender.

- A potential victim/target.

- The absence of a capable guardian.

Where all three of these factors exist simultaneously a crime event is likely to occur. The three factors determine the where, when and how of criminal action (and often ignore the why). By separating the three areas it is possible to isolate factors that can be controlled in order to stop a crime event from occurring. For example, these theories emphasise the importance of the police as capable guardians performing a 'scarecrow function' as well as the need to link policing strategies to broader attempts to reduce crime (see Chapter 6).

REFLECTIVE TASK

Choose three types of crime and, for each, think about how a motivated offender, suitable target and lack of capable guardian might coincide in time and space and think about the various ways in which the lack of capable guardian could be substituted for a capable guardian in order to prevent the occurrence of each of the three crimes you have chosen to consider.

Broken Windows and signal crimes

The most well-known New Right perspective is the Broken Windows thesis (Wilson and Kelling, 1982). According to Wilson and Kelling if 'broken windows' are not repaired in a neighbourhood then others will soon be broken. These signs of disorder, or 'signal crimes', must be dealt with swiftly otherwise more crime will inevitably follow. The priority for public order or 'beat' policing is to foster community pride through informal and local forms of social control that improve the quality of life in an area and restore a sense of order. Wilson and Kelling proposed that the police should increase their presence on the streets and increase their levels of intervention with non-criminal behaviour. This includes moving along groups of children, monitoring derelict properties, and stopping people dropping litter or making excessive amounts of noise.

In an earlier piece of work, *Crime and Human Nature* (1985), Wilson, alongside Herrnstein this time, identified what he believed to be the underlying causes of crime that led to the collapse of moral and social authority in these neighbourhoods. According to Wilson and Herrnstein, crime rates were affected by:

- shifts in the age structure of the population (namely, more young men);

- changes in the benefits offered by crime;

- broad social and cultural changes affecting individual or collective social control.

Therefore, the aim of the criminal justice system was to target these three factors in an effort to reduce the harm caused by widespread offending behaviour. The emphasis placed upon young people and informal social controls represented the beginning of the focus upon anti-social behaviour and the criminalisation of uncivil or socially unacceptable behaviour. Wilson and Kelling believed that anti-social behaviour laid the conditions for future criminality and that the only way to stop crime was through making early interventions with these individuals and communities. High levels of crime were to be blamed upon the weakened authority of key social institutions, such as the family, schools, the police, the criminal justice system and organised religion, which needed to be restored. Symbolic crime control measures, such as tough policing and punitive sentencing policies, were needed to re-assert the values of the law-abiding majority.

REFLECTIVE TASK

Why do New Right theorists blame high levels of crime on the weakened authority of families, schools and religious institutions?

The polarisation of left wing conflict theories and right wing consensus theories was a key characteristic of criminology in the UK during the 1970s, but as the decade came to a close, a new theoretical perspective emerged which would combine elements of both conflict and consensus perspectives in order to provide a more holistic and 'realistic' response to the problem of crime.

Left Realism

Left Realism provides a more grounded theoretical perspective on crime that retains the traditional Marxist analysis of the function of capitalism and the social construction of crime but aims to provide practical solutions to problems of crime and disorder. Left Realists note the relative autonomy of the police from the state (see Chapter 3), extensive public support for many police functions and the impact of rapid social change during the 1960s and 1970s on the complexity of the police role. These ideas originated from British criminologists working in the 1970s and 1980s who believed that the radical left had to adapt its thinking in order to be more realistic about the problems presented by crime. Hence, Left Realism:

- left = tough on the causes of crime;

- realism = tough on (the reality of) crime (problems).

Many of the Left-Realist criminologists, such as John Lea and Jock Young (1984), had their roots in the radical Marxist perspective of criminology, but they deliberately sought to remove themselves from this ideological tradition. The Left Realists absorbed some of the ideas from Conservative, right wing criminologists with their emphasis on crime control and situated them within a framework that also emphasised the need to address issues of poverty, unemployment and poor housing. At the heart of the Left-Realist perspective is an acknowledgement that crime is a very real source of suffering for the poor and the vulnerable, particularly in socially excluded urban areas in towns and cities and that crime rates are influenced by four interacting factors that make up 'a square of crime'.

1. The police and other agencies of social control.

2. The public.

3. Offenders.

4. Victims.

Inspired by the ideas of the Left Realists, Tony Blair's 'New' Labour government expanded the previous Conservative focus upon being 'tough on crime' to include being tough on the 'causes of crime' when they were elected in 1997. This meant that all the sides of Lea and Young's square could now be covered. While being 'tough on crime' emphasised the importance of treating offenders as free-willed, rational actors, being 'tough on causes' also put the focus on background factors, related to strain and social structure, that pushed an individual into offending.

REFLECTIVE TASK

Rather than providing new insights into offending behaviour and response to it, Left Realists bring together a range of criminological theories in an attempt to provide a holistic explanation of crime. Which of the theories that have been previously outlined in this chapter can you identify within Left Realism?

Post-modernism

In the UK, the focus on crime prevention from the 1980s onwards involved a new 'moral' agenda that asserted the responsibilities of individual citizens, private companies and voluntary agencies in combating the problem of crime. This process involved a recognition that the state could no longer be solely relied upon to protect the public from crime. All members of society were encouraged to become active citizens and play their part in addressing problems in their neighbourhood. This 'responsibilisation' of citizens (Garland, 1996) led to a shift in focus from crime and offenders (looking at the causes of crime) to crime prevention and community safety (finding 'solutions' to crime problems). This re-structuring of response to crime involved a post-modern, pluralisation of policing (see Chapter 6) where the police's previous monopoly of control over policing services fragmented and was increasingly undertaken by a multitude of policing providers from the statutory, voluntary and commercial sectors.

Tension between policing, security and order maintenance at the local, national and international levels has made it more difficult to police contemporary societies. Enhanced awareness of uncertainty and risk under the conditions of late modernity (see Chapter 8) has led to a broadening of the problems faced by policing agencies. In the 'information age', policing has become increasingly dependent upon the production of intelligence and the role of the police as 'knowledge workers' (Ericson and Haggerty, 1997). In these circumstances, crime and deviance are increasingly perceived to be technical problems that require management through *procedures and technologies – classification schemes, probability calculations etc.* (Ibid., page 39).

Both the New Right and Left Realists were targeted by different forms of criticism from post-modernist scholars. Post-modernists saw the Left-Realist desire to create of a total picture of crime as an illusion when all knowledge is situated and partial. Similarly, post-modernists critiqued New Right communitarian ideas by noting the absence of traditional communities in late modern societies as well as the manufactured nostalgia of the 1950s language and imagery used to evoke emotional responses from members of the public. This post-modernist critique led to a fragmentation of criminological thought from the 1990s onwards which encouraged the evolution of a multi-disciplinary subject that incorporated ideas from sociology, political science, law, geography and economics. The discipline of criminology has subsequently broken up into a multitude of sub-disciplines that either are attached to criminal justice professions, such as policing, or use specific analytical tools to interpret the problem of crime and responses to it (e.g. crime science, green criminology, cultural criminology, critical criminology, and many, many more).

PRACTICAL TASK

Having read an introduction to a range of different criminological theories, which of the theories do you think fits most closely with your perspective on the causes of crime and responses to it?

The theories should help you explain why different offences might take place. Have a look at the following and identify which theories are most useful in explaining why these offences take place.

- Domestic violence.

- Drug use.

- Graffiti and vandalism.

- Burglary.

- Car crime.

Have a look at the good practice guidance on the Crime Reduction Partnership website (www.crp-news.com/htm/subjectsgood_practice.htm) which suggests a number of policing and crime reduction strategies to combat these offences. Which criminological theories are the organisations on the website using to understand why these offences occur?

CASE STUDY

Everytown has received an increased amount of coverage in the local and regional media about its crime and disorder problems. As Everytown's new policing and community safety officer, you have been tasked with designing a response to these problems on behalf of the local residents. Everytown is an area of mixed tenure properties with predominantly local authority tenants. Residents have complained about groups of anti-social young people, drug misuse and dealers operating from flats and phone boxes. There is also concern about a growth in the amount of criminal damage and graffiti. Stories about low-level offences are now being reported in the local newspaper on a regular basis and this has led to a rise in fear of crime among Everytown's residents.

- *Which criminological theories help you explain why there might have been an increase in crime?*

CASE STUDY CONTINUED

- *Which criminological theories help you explain why fear of crime has increased?*

- *In your opinion, what sort of policing response is needed to manage the problems that the area is facing?*

C H A P T E R   S U M M A R Y

One of the most common questions raised by policing students when studying criminological theory and methodological approaches is concerned with their relevance to twenty-first century operational policing. Yet, criminological theories help us understand how governments, criminal justice agencies and individuals think about crime and how they devise their responses to this problem. Equally, different methodological approaches are linked to specific theoretical perspectives and the construction of a particular vision of crime and criminal justice agencies. The initial preference for ethnographic study of the police was driven by a desire to qualitatively understand the social world that the police worked in, though this was gradually replaced with a greater quantitative focus on interviews, surveys and questionnaires which was preferred by administrative criminologists and which measured efficiency and effectiveness within the Police Service.

There are good historical reasons for this. Prior to the 1990s there was a noticeable distance between the UK police and criminological researchers which was characterised by significant mutual mistrust. In part, this was due to a general criminological focus on negative aspects of policing but also due to an insularity within police culture that kept out outsiders. This situation has changed quite dramatically and two schools of police researchers have emerged in the twenty-first century. These two areas are not mutually exclusive but broadly include the following.

- *Critical criminologists* – whose main function involves critical inquiry of the police role.

- *Police-friendly researchers* – who include in-house police researchers or researchers from police-friendly institutions and are policy or strategy-focused.

The emergence of police studies as a distinct area of study in universities has re-enforced this split with departments often being populated with criminologists from one school of thought rather than a mixture of the two. Consequently, the development of police studies has split along the traditional criminological contours of consensus and conflict theories. The rest of this book introduces you to the influence criminology has had on the development of policing (and, more recently, vice versa), beginning with analysis of the establishment of the 'new' police.

There are a multitude of textbooks on criminological theories that will allow you to develop your understanding of the different theoretical perspectives further.

Roger Hopkins Burke (2009) *An Introduction to Criminological Theory* is now in its third edition.

Tim Newburn's (2008) *Handbook of Policing* (2nd edition) provides an excellent overview of the broad subject of policing with contributions from many of the leading scholars in the field.

Michael Rowe's (2008) *Introduction to Policing* also provides an up-to-date introduction to the subject which makes more explicit links with developments in criminological theory.

Eugene McLaughlin's (2007) *The New Policing* provides a comprehensive review of the most relevant criminological literature on policing as well as providing a sophisticated guide to contemporary changes in forms of policing and the potential futures that lie ahead.

Banton, M (1964) *The Policeman in the Community*. London: Tavistock.

Chan, J (1996) Changing police culture. *British Journal of Criminology*, **36**(1): 109–34.

Cohen, A (1955) *Delinquent Boys: The Culture of the Gang*. Illinois: Free Press.

Cohen, S (1985) *Visions of Social Control*. Cambridge: Polity.

Cohen, L and Felson, M (1979) Social Inequality and Predatory Criminal Victimization: An Exposition and Test of a Formal Theory. *American Sociological Review*, **44**(4): 588–608.

Downes, D (1966) *The Delinquent Solution*. London: Hutchinson.

Durkheim, E (1933 originally 1893) *The Division of Labour in Society*. Glencoe: Free Press.

Ericson, R and Haggeaty, K (1977) *Policing the Risk Society*. Oxford: Clarendon Press.

Ferrell, J, Hayward, K and Young, J (2008) *Cultural Criminology: An Invitation*. London: Sage.

Fielding, N (1988) *Joining Forces: Police Training, Socialisation and Occupational Competence*. London: Routledge.

Foucault, M (1977) *Discipline and Punish*. London: Penguin.

Garland, D (1996) The Limits of the Sovereign State. *British Journal of Criminology*, **36**(4): 445–71.

Holdaway, S (1984) *Inside the British Police*. Oxford: Blackwell.

Hopkins Burke, R (2009) *An Introduction to Criminological Theory*, 3rd edition. Cullompton: Willan.

Lea, J and Young, J (1984) *What Is to Be Done about Law and Order? Crisis in the Eighties*. London: Penguin.

Lemert, E (1951) *Social Pathology: Systematic Approaches to the Study of Sociopathic Behaviour*. New York: McGraw-Hill.

Matza, D (1964) *Delinquency and Drift*. New York: John Wiley and Sons.

McLaughlin, E (2007) *The New Policing*. London: Sage.

Merton, R (1938) Social Structure and Anomie. *American Sociological Review*, **3**(5): 672–82.

Newburn, T (2008) *Handbook of Policing*, 2nd edition. Cullompton: Willan.

Park, R and Burgess, E (1925) *The City*. Chicago: Chicago University Press.

Reiner, R (2010) *The Politics of the Police*, 4th edition. Oxford: Oxford University Press.

Rowe, M (2008) *Introduction to Policing*. London: Sage.

Shaw, C and McKay, H (1942) *Juvenile Delinquency in Urban Areas*. Chicago: Chicago University Press.

Waddington, P A J (1999) Police (Canteen) Sub-culture: An Appreciation. *British Journal of Criminology*, **39**(2): 287–309.

Wilson, J and Herrnstein, R (1985) *Crime and Human Nature: The Definitive Study of the Causes of Crime*. New York: Free Press.

Wilson, J and Kelling, G (1982) Fixing Broken Windows. *The Atlantic Monthly*, **249**(3): 29–38.

2   Policing and society

Introduction

This chapter explores the very earliest forms of policing in England and Wales prior to the establishment of the Metropolitan Police force in London in 1829. The chapter looks at the evolution of the 'new police' throughout the nineteenth century and connects this to broader changes in society at that time. The chapter introduces students to the value of historical analysis in interpreting the role of police in society, be that in the past, the present or the future. The chapter also returns to the theoretical perspectives that were introduced in the first chapter of the book and uses them to explain why the police institution developed during this specific historical period.

A brief introduction is provided to policing structures and institutions prior to the modern police force. The organisational development and growth of policing throughout the nineteenth century is subsequently outlined and two dominant criminological explanations for the emergence of the police at this time are introduced. This section explains the importance of criminological theory as an analytical tool which helps us interpret historical developments in policing and criminal justice. The final section provides links with the third chapter and compares the role and function of the police in the nineteenth and twenty-first centuries.

Policing before the police

Prior to undertaking any historical analysis, it is important to clarify the important distinctions between the terms 'policing' and 'the police'. 'Policing' as a process, or a mode of social control, must be separated from 'the police' as an institution who are responsible for specific policing activities (Johnston and Shearing, 2003). Policing as a mode of social control pre-dates the existence of the police institution in England and Wales. It is the emergence of the police institution in the nineteenth century that is our concern here and the shift from ad hoc policing arrangements in which a multitude of, often, private policing agencies competed for work to a single, dominant professional police force paid for by central and local government. The police institution is separated from most other policing agencies, for example private security, through the legal powers it provides its personnel with, most significantly, to use physical force (Bittner, 1975). Yet again, the monopoly over legal force that helps us define the police institution is coming under threat (see Chapter 6) and this makes an understanding of the pre-history of the police institution even more important.

The idea of policing as a necessary social function emerged during the Middle Ages although it was only ever organised at the local level. Knights of the shire, local constables (a term introduced by the Normans), local Watches (set up in the Statute of Winchester 1285), and justices of the peace (a role codified under the Justice of the Peace Act, 1361) all carried out policing functions. These roles were mainly undertaken by volunteers who would have felt compelled by a sense of civic duty (and occasionally fines and the threat of force) to carry out these roles. These policing structures remained in place until the middle of the eighteenth century when public concern about rising crime and disorder encouraged debate about policing and, more broadly, criminal justice. Across society, questions were being asked about the effectiveness of traditional modes of deterrence such as capital punishment and transportation. A view slowly developed among the ruling classes that the existing structure of amateur volunteers operating at the parish level was unable to manage the new problems of crime and disorder presented by rapid urbanisation and rising discontent among an often impoverished workforce.

By 1750, policing was carried out by a mixture of parish constables and night watchmen. Watchmen patrolled a short beat or stood in a kiosk at night time. They were paid a relatively low wage, which meant that the quality of the personnel was variable. Parish Constables were tasked with following up complaints from victims and investigating crimes. The constables were generally educated and literate and were held to account by local justices of the peace. The parish constables did not receive a wage but they claimed expenses and rewards for successfully prosecuting criminals on behalf of victims, hence the name 'thief-takers'. The most famous of these were the Bow Street runners, formed by the novelist and magistrate Henry Fielding in 1750, who were London's first professional team of investigators.

REFLECTIVE TASK

- *Why is policing regarded as a key component of functioning societies?*
- *What do you think are the different factors that would have encouraged people in the Middle Ages to carry out a policing role?*

The threat to social order

Henry Fielding's (1751) An *Enquiry into the Cause of the Late Increase of Robberies and Other Writings* highlighted the need for a more systematic preventive response to the problem of crime. Fielding saw the main cause of crime as being the increased wealth of the lower classes which had released them from their previous dependence on the ruling classes and given rise to decadent interests such as the consumption of alcohol, gambling and other disreputable leisure pursuits. According to Fielding, a new mode of government was required to regulate public morality and to restore authority and order before this thirst for licentiousness and vice spread throughout society. Fielding likened the threat posed by the lower classes to a disease that would spread throughout the social body, *for bad habits are as infectious by example, as the plague itself by contact* (1988, page 77). Therefore, *the business of the politician is to prevent the contagion from spreading to the useful part of mankind* (Ibid., pages 83–84).

Fielding's ideas were supported by another magistrate Patrick Colquhoun who proposed in his *Treatise on the Police of the Metropolis* (1796) that a new organised system of police was required to stop crime increasing in London. Colquhoun also made links between increased wealth and a rise in immoral behaviour and placed the temptations present for the newly urbanised London population at the heart of his argument. Colquhoun's neo-classical perspective on crime meant that he viewed the social body as being seduced into vice and a potential cycle of crime and deviance that would render them useless members of society. Thus, it was the job of good government to provide sufficient deterrence from this temptation and to protect the public from themselves!

The 'new police' and the birth of criminological theory

The ideas of Fielding and Colquhoun can be linked to those of the eighteenth century philosopher Cesare Beccaria (1738–94), and the British social reformer Jeremy Bentham (1748–1832). Beccaria saw existing systems of justice in the eighteenth century as being inherently inefficient in managing problems of crime and disorder. The prevalence of often arbitrary corporal and capital punishments meant that responses to crime were unsystematic and had little deterrent effect on the population. Beccaria's ideas utilised the social contract theories that became popular during the enlightenment period and which still underpin many neo-classical criminal justice systems today. Social contract theories view people as rational individuals who are inherently selfish and in potential conflict with each other as they pursue their individual desires. In response to this potential conflict, it is the role of government to offer a social contract through which each individual relinquishes a small part of their liberty in return for the protection of the state against the threats posed by other individuals to life and property. Through this process modern, civil societies are created.

Beccaria emphasised the importance of increasing the chances of apprehending offenders and the subsequent certainty of their punishment for wrongdoing as part of this process. Thus, the security of society was achieved through the pursuit and prosecution of offenders and the success of this process deterred others from committing the same (rational) acts. Bentham was a follower of Beccaria who was influenced by the philosophical ideas of John Locke (1632–1704) and his emphasis upon the utilitarian nature of justice. This meant that the aim of good government should be 'the greatest happiness for the greatest number'. Locke blamed criminal behaviour upon poor socialisation rather than an innate tendency to offend. Offenders were not to be viewed as monsters but instead as people who lacked the self-discipline to control their passions. As people were rational creatures who sought pleasure and attempted to avoid pain, this instinct could be moulded in order to create human beings who were happy to comply with the law and society's wider interests.

Bentham is best known for his design of a prison model known as the 'Panopticon' that provided the inspiration for Pentonville prison in London. The Panopticon was made up of a circular honeycomb of cells that surrounded a central inspection tower from which each prisoner could be seen by the prison guards. Bentham proposed that permanent surveillance would help to regulate the behaviour of offenders and reform them into good citizens. Bentham saw the Panopticon as a model that could be duplicated throughout society in order to regulate the behaviour of all citizens in line with the needs of the authorities. Thus, the aims of the preventive police for Colquhoun and Fielding were to provide direct surveillance of problem areas and individuals while also encouraging members of the public to look out for crime and to report it to them.

Modern theories of social control (Foucault, 1977; Cohen, 1985; Garland, 2001) cite this model of regulating and disciplining the behaviour of individuals as providing a significant shift in thinking about the role of criminal justice in society. An old system of often random and brutal punishments was beginning to give way and being replaced by a more efficient and humane system that focused on the pro-active prevention of crime ahead of the retrospective punishment of individuals. This shift in thinking also helps us understand the more recent growth in CCTV, speed cameras and other forms of surveillance which aim to regulate our behaviour by offering constant surveillance of the streets.

Colquhoun's neo-classical views influenced the thinking of the Marine Police who were formed in 1798 with the principal aim of establishing an 'unremitting watch' over the Thames docks. In 1800, this commercial organisation was taken over by central government and became the Thames River Police, as recognition of their success in preventing crime from boats on the docks. The Thames River Police were supervised by magistrates and provided a model for the later establishment of the Metropolitan Police through their preventive focus on deterrence through patrol. Underpinning this remained a perspective, emanating out from the ruling classes, and grounded in Beccarian and Benthamite thinking, that a newly emancipated public were faced with temptations and seductions which were too strong for them to resist. The advent of a new and permanent professional police was to be the governmental response that would restore both moral and social order.

CASE STUDY

The idea that the public can have too much wealth and freedom prevails today. Have a look at the following articles. One hundred years after Fielding, Engels paints a similar picture of drunken debauchery in mid-nineteenth century Manchester.

> *I have rarely come out of Manchester on such an evening without meeting numbers of people staggering and seeing others lying in the gutter. On Sunday evening the same scene is usually repeated, only less noisily. (Engels, 1845, page 127)*

Evoking similar concerns, the introduction of the Licensing Act 2003 provoked this vitriolic response from The Daily Mail.

> *Supermarkets began selling alcohol cheaper than bottled water... but police warned it was falling into the hands of the young who used it to 'preload' before going drunk to town centres... Rank and file police say the combination of late opening and 'preloading' has stretched their resources to breaking point, warning that some town centres have been turned into the 'wild west'. (Slack, 2010)*

- *What are the causes of the social problems outlined above?*

- *What role should the police play in combating these threats to social order?*

Why did the 'new police' emerge at this time?

Following a similar path to Colquhoun's Thames River Police, Fielding's Bow Street Runners received statutory recognition in the 1792 Middlesex Justices' Act and became a state-funded policing agency. While the Bow Street Runners retained many similarities with previous thief-takers, their institutional arrangements made them innovative: investigators were paid by magistrates who, in turn, were funded by central government. The 'new police' would separate themselves from the magistrates system, and become accountable to the Home Secretary, yet Fielding's runners and Colquhoun's river police provided important precedents to the 'new police' and both would eventually be subsumed into the new structures of police governance in 1839.

Continued concern about the problem of social order led to four separate parliamentary select committees discussing the possibility of a new police institution between 1812 and 1828. Concerns about threats to individual liberty dominated these debates but the persistence of political radicalism coupled with statistics produced by Peel on rises in crime and some deft political manoeuvring ensured that the new Metropolitan Police of London were active by September 1829. Peel's political know-how was also evident in the appointment of the first two police commissioners. Sir Richard Mayne was a barrister who was able to emphasise the police's duty to the law and their institutional independence while Colonel Charles Rowan's links with the military provided a reminder that the maintenance of social order was a core police function.

The establishment of the Metropolitan Police in 1829 by the Home Secretary Sir Robert Peel represented a compromise from his earlier attempts to form a national police force. Attempts to establish a national police force generated significant resistance from local authorities who were fearful of a militarised, continental-style model of policing that would impact upon local autonomy and could be misused by a repressive government. Furthermore, Peel had to exclude the powerful City of London from the Metropolitan Police's new jurisdiction in order to see the legislation through parliament, although the 'square mile' would establish its own police force a decade later.

The establishment of the Metropolitan Police has, thus far, been portrayed as a response to urban unrest and public disorder. Yet, while evidence of crime and disorder confirmed the need for a policing function, they did not drive the police reform agenda. The Victorian era was characterised by the increasing need for a professional local administration to replace county administration that was still run by local squires and justices of the peace. Thus, the development of the 'new police' is as much associated with the local government reform movement of this time as with specific causes of unrest such as the 1780 Gordon Riots and the 1819 Peterloo Massacre. Criminological perspectives on the evolution of the 'new police' have been dominated by two schools of thought. The orthodox model dominated established thinking up until the 1970s when it was challenged by revisionists who called into question some of the traditional assumptions that existed in established police history. The next two sections provide an introduction to the models.

The orthodox explanation

The orthodox explanation of the establishment of the Police Service states that the formation of the professional police was an administrative response to changing social and economic circumstances such as the growth of cities and the population shifts this produced. One of the most famous exponents of the orthodox viewpoint was Charles Reith who wrote a number of police histories throughout the 1930s and 1940s. Reith (1948) described the 'new police' as being a response to public demand for greater social order necessitated by the presence of political unrest, social disorder and rises in street crime. Indeed, Reith suggests that public support for the police was generated by their success in combating burglary and street disorder and is evidenced by the calls for new police forces to be set up around the country after the establishment of the London Metropolitan Police.

It is difficult to confirm Reith's view that there was a rise in crime at this time. Emsley (1996, page 25) notes that the statistics used by Peel were dubious; yet it is clear that there was a view among the ruling classes that crime and disorder were perceived to be a problem. The demise of transportation to North America and the decreasing faith in capital punishment meant that new modes of crime control were in demand. The persistent presence of street disorder and political radicalism, often inspired by the American and French revolutions, generated a paranoia among the ruling class that working-class activism could disrupt international trade and even present a revolutionary threat. Concern about political unrest and rising crime increased demand for a more efficient criminal justice system and it was against this backdrop that support for the establishment of a police force was built.

The orthodox viewpoint is underpinned by a belief that there is a general consensus across society about what the police should be doing and how they should do it. This is evident in the early police histories which view the establishment of a professional police force as a product of forward thinking reformers. While there was significant resistance to the idea of a centralised police force, not least from the threat of adopting a continental, militarised system, support for reforms of the existing watch system grew in the early part of the nineteenth century. The main aim of this reform was to develop a more efficient system of crime prevention through the development of a paid police force that would replace the focus on detection. The existing structure of constable, watchman and justice of the peace placed too much emphasis on the victim, requiring them to pay a fee for a thief-taker to track down an offender. This system provided little incentive for constables to deal with low-level crime and was subject to corruption.

When Robert Peel was appointed as Home Secretary in 1822 he sought to restore public support for the criminal justice system by making it more efficient through a process of centralisation. Thus, the creation of the Metropolitan Police in 1829 involved a shift in responsibility for policing from the London authorities to central government. Views on the role of government were also changing. Good government had previously been interpreted as the state playing a minimal role so as not to interfere with the rights of citizens. Political unrest and rising crime had changed this, and governmental security was increasingly being perceived by the ruling classes as their best form of protection from the dangerous classes. From here we can see how the police's role as protectors of life and property developed as the protection of these rights came to outweigh the rights of minimum interference from the state.

The orthodox, or consensus, perspective is supported by responses from parliament and the media to the creation of the 'new police' which acknowledged the need for radical reform as well as the way in which the Metropolitan Police model spread out into the provinces throughout the first half of the nineteenth century. According to Emsley (1996) the consensus of support for the 'new police' was firmly in place by the mid-nineteenth century and remained strong up until the late 1950s when criticism of the police developed in the wake of a number of scandals that ultimately resulted in the 1962 Royal Commission on the Police.

REFLECTIVE TASK

- *Why did the ruling classes support the establishment of the 'new police'?*

- *Why was the City of London not included in Peel's plans for the 'new police'?*

The revisionist explanation

While it is clear that the 'new police' gained substantial support in a relatively short period of time the long process of police reform throughout the middle part of the nineteenth century demonstrates that significant resistance existed across the country to the establishment of Peel's model of policing. The early histories of the police in England and Wales were written by chief constables, politicians and other establishment figures who portrayed the evolution of policing as a logical and rational development for a modern, civilised society. This perspective is challenged by the revisionists who focus upon the different police structures that were constructed across the country and the ongoing mistrust that existed towards the idea of a centralised police force. The revisionist explanation views the creation of the police in England and Wales as a political response to the perceived threat presented by an organised industrial working class coupled with additional concerns about the growth of revolutionary movements in Europe. Therefore, the role of the police should be understood as a mechanism to discipline the emerging working class to ensure that they were productive and met the aims of industrial capital. This was a particular concern in urban areas where large-scale organisation and demonstrations meant that the working class was perceived as a threat to the position of the ruling elite.

The military had shown themselves to be unable to control the urban poor during the 1780 Gordon Riots and the Peterloo Massacre in Manchester in 1819 and this resulted in the search for a more legitimate means of regulating public disorder.

Concern about large public protests coincided with a regulatory drive that targeted the leisure pursuits of the working class. These included drinking, street gambling, cock-fighting, street-fighting and even visiting the theatre (Sheppard, 1971). Reiner (2000) describes how this disciplinary strategy generated antagonism from the new working class that manifested itself in the branding of the 'new police' as the 'blue locusts', the 'raw lobsters' and 'Peel's bloody gang'.

The clearest distinction between the orthodox and revisionist accounts relates to public support for the police. The revisionists, such as Storch (1976) and Cohen (1979), place an emphasis on the enduring nature of public resistance to the police throughout the nineteenth century and beyond. In particular, working-class resistance focused on the policing of social activities and organised political activity. The policing of working-class activism has been visible throughout the police's history from the early Chartists through to the miner's strike in the 1980s and the G8 protests in the twenty-first century. This rejection of police authority was also evident in the resistance to the police that manifested itself in the urban disorders of the late 1950s and early 1980s and which mimicked much of the concern about the coercive nature of the police role in the 1830s and 1840s. Revisionist accounts place great emphasis on the role of the 'new police' being intrinsically tied to the demands of industrial capital and the need to discipline and train the working class. Storch (1976, page 481) describes the 'new police' as 'domestic missionaries' whose role it was 'to mould a labouring class amenable to new disciplines of both work and leisure'.

REFLECTIVE TASK

- *To what extent do you agree with the orthodox and revisionist accounts of the police in England and Wales?*

- *Having read the last two sections, what, in your view, is the core function of the public police?*

Using theory to make sense of developments in policing

Despite their differences, it is clear that the orthodox and revisionist accounts of the birth of the 'new police' have similarities. Both accounts recognise the importance of broader social and economic change as well as the problem of public disorder. Both accounts recognise that support for the police grew throughout the nineteenth century yet they differ about the extent of working-class resistance towards police authority. The key distinction between the two perspectives lies within their interpretations of nineteenth century society. The orthodox model provides a vision of a society where a *consensus* exists among the public about the need for a professional police force. On the other hand, the revisionist model paints a picture of a society in *conflict* with a paranoid ruling class extending their control over a politically agitated and disorderly working class.

These consensus and conflict perspectives are important criminological tools which help us to interpret the actions of policy makers and the police as well as public responses to these developments. For example, it is clear that the concerns of Colquhoun in the late eighteenth century centred on the regulation of the life-styles of working people and their relationship with the ruling class, a viewpoint that supports the conflict perspective. Furthermore, the rise of the 'new police' coincided with an increasingly pervasive perception among the ruling classes that the previous social order had, to some degree, broken down and that new forms of authority were required to restore order. But, Colquhoun's vision of the 'new police' made little impact at the policy level and the Police Service that was established by Peel, Mayne and Rowan rapidly gained public support from large swathes of society, a viewpoint that supports the consensus perspective. This book uses both consensus and conflict perspectives throughout to provide you with a balanced account of developments in policing and to help you develop an insight into the role and function of the police. The book also introduces a number of other competing theoretical perspectives.

For example, viewed from a distance much of the debate that surrounded the establishment and consolidation of the 'new police' revolved around the issue of police governance and whether this should be structured around parish, county or central governmental control. From this perspective, the policing debate focused as much on political philosophy as it did on the management of crime and disorder. Here, it is clear that a shift took place in the thinking of the ruling classes, from a belief in a restricted role for liberal government that would not curtail individual civil liberties to an emphasis upon the protection of life and property inspired by a fear of crime, lax morals and political radicalism. This led to a shift in the ownership of policing taking place with communities relinquishing control over the 'new police' in return for a more efficient and professional system. This was most evident with the Metropolitan Police who reported directly to the Home Secretary while local authorities retained more control over their police forces in the towns and rural areas.

What was new about the 'new police'?

Between 1829 and 1860 new salaried and uniformed police forces were founded across England and Wales. The 'new police' claimed to provide a fair and equitable service to all members of the public irrespective of wealth unlike the previous system of watchmen and constables, although, as the previous section noted, this viewpoint remains open to conjecture. The ethos of the 'new police' represented a distinct break from the responsive thief-takers. Rather than responding to individual incidents the 'new police' aimed to prevent crime and disorder by providing a visible presence on the streets that could deter potential offenders.

Alongside the emphasis on prevention, the other most significant change was the detachment of the police from the London parish authorities and the local community. This meant that rate payers were no longer able to direct police strategy in the way they had previously. Despite the significant changes in governance, there were also significant continuities with the old system of policing. The 'new police' continued with the hierarchical system of supervision and the focus on beat policing that had been developed by the successful watches. Peel attempted to separate his 'new police' from the military by avoiding their colours and creating a blue uniform but his appointment of Colonel Charles Rowan as one of the first two commissioners ensured a direct connection with the military that could utilise their experience of policing social order in the colonies. This was also evident in the military drills that the police undertook as part of their training.

For the rest of the century the role of the 'new police' would focus upon walking a set beat and, because of this, their impact was experienced most vividly by the working classes whose lives revolved around public places. Because of this, resistance to the police from working-class groups often oriented over the right to use the street for work, leisure and sometimes protest. Conversely, the middle classes, who conducted much of their life in private places, rarely came into contact with police officers. Much of the criticism of the 'new police' would be familiar to twenty-first century observers. Complaints were made about the 'new police' being more expensive than their predecessors, about there being insufficient numbers on the street, and about a lack of local control (Rawlings, 2002).

PRACTICAL TASK

Review what you have read so far in this chapter and identify the key differences between the 'new police' and the old system of parish constables, night watchmen and justice of the peace?

Policing town and country

The success of the Metropolitan Police in managing disorder in London during the 1830s coupled with the successful deployment of officers to the provinces to help quell Chartist radicalism gradually increased support for a shift away from the use of parish constables in rural areas. Rural disorder and unrest continued throughout the 1830s and 1840s causing local authorities to look to the capital with increasing envy (Sheppard, 1971). At the same time, the appetite for reform in rural areas was tempered by a fear of rising tax rates and a loss of parish control. Because of this, nineteenth century police legislation was structured around local provision and local control in towns and rural areas that resulted in a multitude of organisational structures and over 200 separate police forces.

The Municipal Corporations Act 1835 provided towns (or boroughs) with a legal obligation to set up a local police force under the supervision of a Watch committee. The Watch committee was made up of elected officials and acted as a precursor of the modern police authority. The Watch committee wrote the rules and regulatory procedures for their force and retained the power to hire, promote and ultimately sack any member of the police force. The focus of the early professional police on low-level street behaviour emanated out of the Watch committee structure through which powerful local figures could direct the police to respond to their concerns. There was little Home Office interference which meant that local power structures influenced how and where policing services were delivered. Over half of the boroughs established a police force in the two years following on from the 1835 Act although there was still substantial resistance in some areas to this perceived centralisation of power.

The Rural Constabulary Act 1839 introduced the 'new police' into the countryside, in part, not only as a response to the continuing threat presented by Chartist radicalism but also to improve the policing of offenders who migrated from one area to another to avoid detection. The county police were overseen by justices of the peace who, meeting only four times a year, had much less influence over policing issues when compared to the Watch committees. Instead, the chief constable played a much more central role in determining police priorities as well as hiring and firing staff. The 1839 legislation was a non-mandatory act, allowing the local authorities to determine whether or not they appointed a police force (and so incurred extra cost), yet the act ultimately paved the way for a permanent force. While the Metropolitan Police Act had broken the principle of local control by making the police answerable to the Home Secretary and not local authorities in London, this centralisation was resisted elsewhere due to concerns that continental-style policing for political purposes might be introduced into England. Because of this, there were a multitude of reasons behind the establishment of county forces relating to cost, perceptions of crime, the extent of disorder and local politics (Rawlings, 2002, pages 132–35). Although 21 counties had taken on board the provisions of the act by 1841, only nine more counties adopted the act over the next 15 years (Ibid., page 137.) Piecemeal legislation followed the 1839 Act in the form of the Parish Constable Act 1842 and The Superintending Constables Act 1850 which provided alternative systems of rural police; however these forces continued to attract criticism for their perceived inefficiency.

The County & Borough Police Act 1856 made local policing mandatory and simultaneously established Her Majesty's Inspectorate of Constabulary (HMIC) as a mechanism through which central government could influence the local provision of policing. This oversight was deemed necessary due to the resistance from the counties and boroughs to the abolition of local controls which resulted in governmental concessions during the passage of the bill through parliament. The Home Office was required to drop clauses that would have given the Home Secretary oversight of police performance in the counties and boroughs and made the chief constable directly accountable to central government (Emsley, 1996, page 54). Alongside the introduction of HMIC, governmental influence over local policing was also maintained through the introduction of an optional grant which would pay up to 25 per cent of the costs of police forces, although this was withheld from the smaller forces as an incentive to merge. This grant was extended to 50 per cent of costs in 1874.

The Local Government Act 1888 further extended central control over the counties through the establishment of Standing Joint Committees (constituting 50 per cent justices of the peace and 50 per cent local councillors) which were dominated by wealthy landowners and tied the police to the political establishment while excluding radical elements. Despite this, the county police forces retained a focus that was different from that of the Metropolitan Police: that is, the county police forces aimed for detection ahead of prevention which was assisted by the better systems of informal social control that existed in rural areas.

Nineteenth-century police legislation established a hotchpotch of provision based around local control that lasted into the middle of the twentieth century. Central control over the police would be enhanced around the two world wars, most obviously through the 1919 Police Act that unified police pay and conditions nationally and led to the creation of the Police Federation. This, in turn, led to the establishment of an official group of chief constables Association of Chief Police Officers (ACPO) who would become increasingly powerful throughout the twentieth century. Recognising this, the Home Office increasingly intervened in the training, recruitment and appointment of this officer class of police leaders to retain some degree of control over policing strategies. Together, the Home Office and chief constables gained increasing amounts of control over the Watch committees who, when dominated by Labour officials, were seen to present a potentially radical threat, particularly in the period immediately after the First World War when concerns about the Bolsheviks were at their peak.

Criminological theories help us make sense of changing police structures, policies and strategies and explain why the establishment and subsequent proliferation of the police institution bore witness to such a complex mixture of consensus and conflict. Both the orthodox and revisionist explanations help us explain why over 200 county and borough police forces came into existence during this period and neither explanation should be regarded as providing some kind of unqualified truth. Criminological theories provide tools with which we can dissect history and use this knowledge to make sense of contemporary developments in policing. The final part of this chapter provides further critical analysis of the development of the police institution and identifies continuities with the police role in the twenty-first century.

The role and function of the 'new police'

Theoretical perspectives provide a prism through which we can see, understand and interpret the past and use this knowledge to make informed judgements about the future. Each perspective we introduce in this book has its own strengths but equally they all have weaknesses. For example, both the orthodox and revisionist perspectives suffer from an overly rationalised view of history where far-sighted reformers devise policy that is implemented by their willing subordinates. The policy-making process is much more complex than this version of history allows and people do not always make decisions for rational reasons. Indeed, people often act to further their own interest with little idea of the ultimate consequences of their actions. Colquhoun's vision for the police was extremely popular, his *Treatise on the Police of the Metropolis* went through seven editions in nine years (Rawlings, 2002), yet his ideas did not dramatically influence policy. Further, the vision that Peel, Mayne and Rowan had of a preventive police gave way to a focus on more reactive measures from the mid-nineteenth century onwards, with many forces retaining or renewing the historical focus on detection (Emsley, 1983). Therefore, it is particularly presumptuous to expect that historical figures had the foresight that 180 years of policing history has provided us with!

An understanding of the social, economic and political conditions that gave rise to the 'new police' helps us make sense of the police mission, both in the twenty-first century and at its inception in 1829. For example, it was Peel's concern about accusations of governmental interference from the 'new police' that encouraged the focus on prevention (Neyroud and Beckley, 2001). Thus, when in 1829 Richard Mayne issued the newly established force with 'General Instructions', they focused on how they would carry out the following three pro-active functions.

1. The prevention of crime.

2. The protection of life and property.

3. The preservation of public tranquillity.

Underpinning these three core functions were Peel's nine principles of good policing that summarised the enduring philosophy of policing by consent. These were most likely to have been written by Richard Mayne, or his co-commissioner Charles Rowan, and were first published by Charles Reith in 1958. Despite this, they are still known as Peel's principles of policing and are discussed in more detail in Chapter 7. British policing was to be non-political, non-partisan, cooperative rather than authoritarian, and its success would be measured by the absence of crime and disorder. Despite this, a connection was quickly made in the minds of the public, the police and government between the police role and crime fighting. This tension between the reactive focus of crime fighting and the pro-active function of preventive policing and order maintenance remains at the heart of debates about the police role today.

More recently, Les Johnston (2000) took up this debate and identified three core police functions for the twenty-first century that operate in different policing contexts. These are as follows.

- *Crime-orientated policing* (*Reactive*) – this is the core business of the public police and involves responding to emergency calls from the public.

- *Community policing* (*Pro-active*) – this remains a core function of the public police role but is increasingly conducted by the public police alongside police community support officers (PCSOs), special constables, city ambassadors, private security personnel and other members of the community.

- *Order maintenance* (*Pro-active*) – this is an increasingly peripheral public police function. The public police remain involved in order maintenance but mainly as a final port of call.

Order maintenance, or the preservation of public tranquillity, as Mayne referred to it, is undertaken by a multitude of agencies such as housing, education, probation, youth offending and local authorities. Order maintenance is provided by anyone who occupies a civic position of authority and includes a range of roles from private security guards to teachers and lollipop ladies. It is clear from Johnston's definitions that the role and function of the public police changes in different contexts as well as across geographical areas and historical periods. This makes an understanding of the historical role of the police essential if we are to make informed judgements about what the police should be doing in the twenty-first century.

Debate about *what a core police function is* continues because in providing a *service* to one section of the community the police may have to use *coercive force* against another section of the community. Hence, the tension between consensus and conflict perspectives. Age, gender, religion, class, race and culture can all influence whether contact with the police is interpreted as a public service or as a threat of coercive force. Added to this, the complexity involved in understanding twenty-first century policing is enhanced by the multitude of roles the police are expected to undertake. The enduring concern with social order and volume crime coupled with the threat of global crime and international terrorism means that the remit of the twenty-first century Police Service includes a range of functions that are now referred to as protective services. These include

> *counter terrorism and extremism; serious organised and cross border crime;*
> *civil contingencies and emergency planning; critical incident management;*
> *major crime (homicide); public order; and strategic roads policing.*
>
> (O'Connor, 2005, page 1)

PRACTICAL TASK

Having read this chapter, try to identify three important similarities and three important differences between the challenges presented to the police in the nineteenth century and the challenges presented to the Police Service today.

C H A P T E R   S U M M A R Y

> *There must be the application of a correct system of police calculated to reach the root and origin of the evil.*
>
> (Colquhoun, 1796, page 358)

The 'new police' of the nineteenth century were established during a period of rapid social change and enhanced paranoia among the ruling classes about the problem of crime and disorder. Public opinion at the time saw the roots of the problem of crime lying within a more general social and moral malaise as well as the collapse of traditional forms of authority. The establishment of the Metropolitan Police in 1829 was part of a broader governmental response to this concern during a historical period that saw widespread parliamentary reform and the gradual establishment of the criminal justice system that we recognise today.

Nearly 200 years of policing history has subsequently invested the police uniform with a cultural value (both positive and negative) that separates police officers from other figures who undertake policing functions such as PCSOs, private security guards and traffic wardens. The professional police force that developed in England and Wales from 1829 onwards has international historical significance as it provided a model that influenced the development of other policing systems, particularly across the British colonies and in the US. The next chapter takes up this focus on the evolution of policing and looks at how the role and function of the 'new police' developed throughout the twentieth century. The chapter also identifies links between the development of the Police Service and our ever-changing perception of the causes of crime and the best ways of controlling it.

FURTHER READING

The most thorough investigation of the origins of the Police Service can be found in Clive Emsley's (1996) *The English Police*. Robert Reiner's (2000) *The Politics of the Police* introduces the orthodox and revisionist explanations of the birth of the police and provides some thoughtful analysis on the strengths and weaknesses of each perspective. Further detail can be found on neo-classical theoretical perspectives in a multitude of texts on criminological theory, with Roger Hopkins Burke (2009) *Introduction to Criminological Theory* being one of the most accessible.

REFERENCES

Bayley, D and Shearing, C (2003) *Governing Security*. London: Routledge.

Bittner, E (1975) *The Functions of the Police in Modern Society*. New York: Aronson.

Cohen, P (1979) Policing the working class city, in Fine, B, Kinsey, R, Lea, J, Picciotto S and Young, J (eds) *Capitalism and the Rule of Law*. London: Hutchinson.

Cohen, S (1985) *Visions of Social Control*. Cambridge: Polity Press.

Colquhoun, P (1796/2010) *A Treatise on the Police of the Metropolis*, 4th edition. London: British Library.

Emsley, C (1983) *Crime and Society in England: 1750–1900*. Harlow: Longman.

Emsley, C (1996) *The English Police: A Political and Social History*. Harlow: Longman.

Engels, F (1845/1987) *The Condition of the Working Class in England*. London: Penguin.

Fielding, H (1751/1988) An Enquiry into the Cause of the Late Increase of Robberies, in Zirker, M (ed) *An Enquiry into the Cause of the Late Increase of Robberies and Other Writings*. Oxford: Clarendon.

Foucault, M (1977) *Discipline and Punish.* London: Penguin.

Garland, D (2001) *The Culture of Control.* Oxford: Oxford University Press.

Hopkins Burke, R (2009) *An Introduction to Criminological Theory*, 3rd edition. Cullompton: Willan.

Johnston, L (2000) *Policing Britain: Risk, Security and Governance.* Harlow: Longman.

Johnston, L and Shearing, C (2003) *Governing Security: Explorations in Policing and Justice.* London: Routledge.

Neyroud, P and Beckley, A (2001) *Policing, Ethics and Human Rights.* Cullompton: Willan.

O'Connor, D (2005) *Closing the Gap: a Review of the 'Fitness for Purpose' of the Current Structure of Policing in England and Wales.* London: HMIC.

Rawlings, P (2002) *Policing: A Short History.* Cullompton. Willan.

Reiner, R (2000) *The Politics of the Police.* Oxford: Oxford University Press.

Reith, C (1948) *A Short History of the British Police.* Oxford: Oxford University Press.

Sheppard, F (1971) *London 1808–70: The Infernal Wen.* London: Secker and Warburg.

Slack, J (2010) An End to 24 Hour Drinking. *Daily Mail Online.* Available online at www.dailymail.co.uk/news/article-1296652/Ministers-pledge-scrap-Labours-failed-licensing-laws.html (Accessed on 24 August 2010).

Storch, R (1976) The policeman as domestic missionary: urban discipline and popular culture in northern England, 1850–80. *Journal of Social History*, **9**(4): 481–509.

USEFUL WEBSITES

Most police websites in the UK provide some historical background to their origins as well as clearly articulated statements on their role and function. The best starting point for Police Service web addresses is www.police.homeoffice.gov.uk. The most detailed official history is provided by the Metropolitan Police Service (www.met.police.uk/history/) although there are plenty of other websites that are worth a read.

www.gmp.police.uk/mainsite/pages/museumhistory.htm

www.learnhistory.org.uk/cpp/met.htm

www.policehistorysociety.co.uk/

3 The evolution of policing in the twentieth century

Introduction

The Police Act 1829 provided legal formalisation of some of the powers necessary for the police to discharge their duties effectively and legitimately. From the mid-nineteenth century, the police enjoyed evermore popular support from the public; a support which they were able to maintain into the twentieth century. From the late 1960s, socio-political changes, including increasing crime rates and a rise in deviant sub-cultures in the UK, led to increased public expectation of the role, function and effectiveness of the police. Widespread community support for the police diminished. Furthermore, the absence of an independent mechanism of accountability between the police and public led to an increased scepticism about the integrity of the police to uphold and enforce the law. This chapter will develop the historical background from the previous chapter and provide valuable context for forthcoming chapters through a discussion of the changing role and function of the Police Service throughout the twentieth century. The chapter discusses the dominant policing philosophies and strategies implemented in the UK to deal with public concerns of increasing crime and deviance from the 1960s and beyond. Throughout the chapter, links will also be made between the development of policing strategy and competing criminological perspectives on offending and deviant behaviour.

Community consensus to community conflict

From the middle of the nineteenth century until the end of the Second World War, the police enjoyed popular and seemingly guaranteed support from the majority of the public. However, by the end of the war, crime rates began to rise and there arose a shortage of police officers. Between 1900 and 1930, crime rates remained low and largely unchanged before a slight rise between 1930 and 1954. From 1954, indictable offences increased significantly and constantly from 9.7 per thousand of population in 1954 to 110 per thousand of population by 1992 (Hicks and Allen, 1999). An increase in predatory crime, particularly theft, burglary and robbery coincided with a concern about 'youth' and a rise in youth offending (Newburn, 2001). From the late 1950s, conflicts arose between and the police and public due to the emergence of youth sub-cultures, the increasing racial diversity of communities and accusations that the police were abusing their legal powers and professional standards.

Conflict between the police and oppressed communities results in mistrust between communities and the police, which undermines the authority and legitimacy of the police. Without legitimacy, it becomes difficult for the police to perform their role as effective crime fighters and to build and maintain public confidence in the police. UK governments have, since the mid-1960s, implemented various reforms of the Police Service to create and sustain relations between the police and the public they serve. Some of these reforms have been accomplished through the implementation of legislative reform as well as non-legislative political directives such as those establishing minimum policing standards, measurable targets and pledges and compacts between the police and public.

PRACTICAL TASK

Have a look at the website www.statistics.gov.uk/hub/crime-justice/index.html to gain an insight into public attitudes towards the police and consider how satisfaction with the police might be improved.

Police Act 1964

To improve accountability and governance of the police force, the government established a Royal Commission on the Police. Although some officers argued that police work could not be done effectively within professional and legal rules, the commission's proposals on accountability and complaints related to the police were implemented in the Police Act 1964. This legislation aimed to establish a new mode of governance for the police (rather than maintaining its integrity to police via its 'professional' standards), improve accountability between the police and the public, provide some form of independent scrutiny of the police and create a legally recognised governance structure. Under the provisions of the 1964 Act, authority over the police was re-distributed from local authorities and local Watch committees to a tri-partite system of governance comprising the Home Secretary, local police authorities and local chief constables. This remains the formal basis for the system of police governance in England and Wales.

This change in governance structure of the police coincided with calls to transform the organisation of police work. Emerging youth sub-cultures, decreasing community cohesion, onset of recession and increasing unemployment were attributed as the cause of an increase in crime and the police were beginning to lose the support and legitimacy from the public that they had, for so long, enjoyed. Many communities were also seen as under-policed, not only because of rising crime but also because of a shortage of serving police officers.

PRACTICAL TASK

Of the three elements in the tri-partite structure (Home Secretary, chief constable and police authorities), police authorities are expected to hold the police to account at the local (or community) level (you can find out more about police authorities at: http://rds.homeoffice.gov.uk/rds/pdfs2/rdsolr3703.pdf).

Rise of youth sub-culture

Youth sub-cultures are sometimes known as 'counter-culture' because the attitudes, beliefs, customs and values held by those engaged in a specific sub-culture are seen to be in direct opposition to those held by 'mainstream' society. The emergence of youth culture movements in the 1970s, such as Mods, Rockers, Skinheads, Far Left political activists and Far Right Fascist groups, was linked with widespread violence, hooliganism (particularly football hooliganism), vandalism and anti-social behaviour. As threatening to public safety and social order as an increase in any of these behaviours is, Cohen (1973) argued that in some circumstances, the public and media reaction to behaviour that is perceived to threaten societal values creates 'folk devils' of those pursuing the behaviour and 'moral panic' across society. According to Cohen (ibid., page 1):

Societies appear to be subject, every now and again, to periods of moral panic. A condition, episode, person or group of persons emerges to become defined as a threat to societal values and interests. In situations of moral panics, the police must act to satisfy the public that they are doing their job properly.

PRACTICAL TASK

Find some examples of how deviants or offenders have been represented in the media as folk devils and consider what impact this has had on public perceptions of policing.

Cohen (1973) identified that the media portrayal of deviancy is a leading element in both the public's identification of 'folk devils' and the propensity for the actions of a particular group of people to promote a 'moral panic'.

Media representations of policing

Successive sweeps of the British Crime Survey reveal that the public are unacquainted with numerous aspects of the criminal justice system and rely on the media for their information (Mawby, 2002). The public's image of the police is often influenced by media representations in factual and fictional media sources.

Representations in fictional media

PRACTICAL TASK

List as many fictional books, magazines or television programmes about policing as you can think of and consider how the police are portrayed and whether these portrayals are accurate.

Robert Reiner recognised that since the mid-nineteenth century, crime and detective fiction has been a prominent part of media output. He argues that the fictional media portray the police in a largely unrealistic way, particularly from the late 1950s onwards (Reiner, 2000). Before then, television programmes such as *The Blue Lamp* and *Dixon of Dock Green* portrayed PC George Dixon as the local friendly bobby (see Reiner, 2006). Fictional representations generally portray the police and their work in a favourable light, but these portrayals are often misrepresentative of real policing.

In fictional programmes, crimes are nearly always successfully cleared up and the offender admits to the crime in response to the clever and cunning questioning skills of the investigating detective, leading to unrealistic expectations of the police under the *assumption that crime can be cleared up routinely in half an hour minus commercial breaks* (Reiner, 2006, page 269). In reality, only 2 per cent of all offences reported in victim surveys result in a conviction and few of these clear-ups are actually the result of skilful detection (Reiner, 2006, page 268). Fictional media also portray police work as exciting, fast-moving and dangerous. In reality, the role and function of the police is a little different to that portrayed by the media (see Bayley, 2005; Waddington and Wright, 2010).

Representations in factual media

The police and media appear to have a reciprocal relationship based upon the need of the media for news stories related to policing because crime stories are newsworthy owing to the publics' enduring fascination with crime and because the police often need the media to convey information to the public. Reiner (2000) claims that the police and media organisations have a troubled relationship and the police largely mistrust the media despite being portrayed in a generally positive light. Sir Robert Mark, former Chief Commissioner of the Metropolitan Police, once described the relationship between the police and media as an enduring, if not ecstatically happy, marriage (Reiner, 2006, page 259). Media interest in policing began in the 1920s due to increased competition between print media organisations and the creation of informal arrangements to buy news stories from the police (Chibnall, 1977). From the end of the 1930s, this relationship changed and cooperation between journalists and police officers developed. From the late 1950s, relationships between the police and media were less assured as the media reported rising crime rates, the negative impact of reduction on foot patrols in favour of car patrols and a number of scandals about police malpractice, deviance and corruption (Mawby, 2002).

The integrity and legitimacy of the Police Service, which had so far been guaranteed through its unquestioned professionalism, came under intense examination. First, in 1956 and 1959, disciplinary and legal proceedings were brought against the Chief Constables of Brighton, Cardiganshire, and Worcestershire Constabularies. Although all three were acquitted, the trial judge stated that *without a change in the leadership of the force, the judiciary would feel unable to believe evidence from Brighton police*. Concerns were also raised about the lack of independent scrutiny of complaints made against the police given it was the police who investigated complaints against themselves. In 1958, this issue also served to undermine the professionalism of the police following allegations that they failed to properly investigate allegations that they had beaten up a young boy in Thurso, Scotland. More serious allegations against the police arose in 1961 with allegations that a detective from the Metropolitan Police planted false evidence on suspects (Reiner, 2000).

PRACTICAL TASK

Conduct a search of six media articles about policing and undertake a brief content analysis to identify the different portrayals of the police in each of the news stories you select. In particular, consider whether the stories portray the police positively or negatively.

Stories of police corruption and malpractice are particularly newsworthy as the media seeks to expose the illicit activities of those who are supposed to uphold the law against the rest of us. Steve Chibnall (1977, page 23) identifies eight *professional imperatives*, which determine whether potential stories are newsworthy, particularly to the newspaper media.

- Immediacy. The story must relate to the present and be instantly reportable.

- Dramatisation. Reports must emphasise action and drama so as to capture the attention of the audience.

- Personalisation. Individuals involved in the stories will receive far more attention than the issues.

- Simplification. Issues are presented in an over-simplistic way on the grounds that a bad news story is one that cannot be absorbed on the first time of reading.

- Titillation. Morality issues such as sex scandals involving well-known personalities.

- Conventionalism. Readers must be able to feel familiar with the context of the stories' settings.

- Structured Access. Stories are often re-enforced by experts (such as criminologists).

- Novelty. Events that are unusual or original are more likely to attract readers' attention.

Unfortunately, many newsworthy stories about the police often damage public confidence in policing and influence public opinion regarding the effectiveness of the police and of policing strategy more generally.

Policing strategy

Since the 1950s, emerging youth sub-cultures, decreasing community cohesion, onset of recession and increasing unemployment have, at some time or other, been attributed as the cause of an increase in crime and deviance. The older and softer community-orientated policing methods that worked so well appeared to be increasingly ineffective in dealing with the different crime and disorder problems of post-war Britain and policing strategy shifted from pro-active and community-orientated to re-active and crime-orientated.

The first re-active and crime-orientated strategy *was Unit Beat Policing*.

Unit Beat Policing

Unit Beat Policing (UBP) was described by the Home Office as the biggest change in fundamental operational police methods since 1829 (Weatheritt, 1986).

- re-active policing;

- localisation of policing;

- the introduction of technology to facilitate easy communication between police officers and police forces;

- the use of police cars to enable the police to patrol large geographical areas quickly with fewer police officers and to facilitate a rapid police response to reports of crime.

Initially, UBP began as an experiment in two towns, Kirby and Accrington in the North of England, before similar experiments were conducted in 30 other towns. The main idea was to enable fewer police officers to patrol large areas by amalgamating larger foot beats into smaller motorised beats to enable fewer police officers to patrol larger areas quickly.

Evidence regarding the success of UBP is quite contradictory. On the one hand, the Home Office Police Research and Planning Unit claimed that everyone, including the public, was pleased with UBP, wherever it was tried, and in Kirkby it had resulted in several arrests and a reduction in vandalism. However, Weatheritt (1986): claims that UBP had given rise to:

- an inappropriate use of resources;

- a perception that beat policing is low in status;

- low police visibility;

- low detection rates;

- poor relations between the police and the public;

- a lack of public cooperation.

Despite the localised nature of the motorised patrol, some claim that it had, in essence, pushed the police into an incident driven, reactive, crime-fighting organisation with a questionable effect on crime or detection rates. According to Orr (1998, page 112),

> *The public's demand for a speeded-up police response during the 1970s and 1980s had seen the universal adoption of the fast car, enhanced technology, and the personal radio. Combined, they ensured a less personal police style. The car provided a physical barrier to community interaction and the personal radio, while producing a vital step forward in communication which no officer would now forfeit, was became increasingly relied upon to deliver instructions on where to call and what to do rather than relying on their personal initiative. Intelligence that would previously have been passed to officers during casual conversation with their community was also lost.*

Despite the change in policing strategy from pro-active to reactive during the 1970s, the police began raising concerns about their capacity to successfully maintain order in an *increasingly turbulent society* (Rawlings, 2002, page 201). During the 1979 general election campaign, the Conservative Party, then in opposition and under the leadership of Margaret Thatcher, placed the restoration of law and order (in addition to economic reform) at the top of their political agenda, where it remained throughout the 1980s. The 1980s saw significant urban disorder and policing policy was increasingly grounded in order maintenance (see below). Much of the disorder was committed primarily by young people and those from low socio-economic groups, who felt increasingly disenfranchised from mainstream society because of unemployment and widening class inequality (Reiner, 2001).

Unemployment, crime and 'strain'

Jones (1998) contends it is dangerous to assume a link between high unemployment and high crime rates. Nevertheless, many studies have been conducted in order to explore this link with variable conclusions. However, the social and economic disadvantage brought on by recession increases the possibility of what American sociologist Robert Merton categorises as anomie (i.e. 'strain'). He argued that strain resulted from the lack of a structured and legitimate means for most people in society to attain material wealth. Merton argued that the desire for material wealth was culturally induced and, although not everyone will be able to attain it, everyone was expected to try and those who did not try risked being categorised as lazy or unambitious (Jones, 1998). Although Merton did not argue that strain occurs only in times of recession, it follows that during recession, the opportunity to attain material wealth through legitimate means diminishes for some and police often warn of a likely increase in personal and property crime. Merton argued that those who are unable to meet the cultural goal of material success can experience one of five reactions under the 'strain' of anomie.

- Conformity.

- Innovation.

- Ritualism.

- Retreatism.

- Rebellion.

The reaction that concerns the police the most during a recession is 'innovation'. Those who experience innovation accept the goal of material wealth but reject the legal and middle-class legitimate means by which to achieve it. According to Merton, the lower classes are most likely to experience difficulties in achieving financial success through legitimate means and so are likely to commit most crime. Hence, innovation is linked to unemployment and economic inequality, which a recession tends to precipitate or advance.

Order maintenance policing

Order maintenance policing, also known as zero tolerance, is primarily grounded in two criminological perspectives: Right Realism and Broken Windows.

Right Realism

Right Realism emerged in the US in 1975 with James Wilson's publication of *Thinking about Crime*. He argued that while increased police patrols and longer prison sentences would have little impact on crime levels, crime is an evil that required a concerted and rigorous response (Hopkins Burke, 2005). Wilson and George Kelling argued that the police are most effectively used to maintain social order, by providing an environment in which criminality is unable to flourish, rather than to reduce crime. According to Hopkins Burke (ibid., page 33):

> *The focus should be less on breaches of the criminal law but more on regulating street life and incivilities – such as prostitution, begging, gang fights, drunkenness and disorderly conduct – which in themselves may not be harmful but in aggregate are detrimental to the community.*

The other fundamental aspect of Wilson and Kelling's argument is that disorder and crime are usually inextricably linked, in a kind of developmental sequence. They explicate this in their Broken Windows thesis, the fundamental basis of which is discussed in Chapter 2.

Zero-tolerance policing

Zero-tolerance policing (ZTP) has its theoretical base in the Broken Windows thesis and is based on three ideas.

- Nipping things in the bud to prevent anti-social elements developing the feeling that they are in charge and to prevent a broken-down and ugly environment of neglect becoming a breeding ground for crime and disorder.
- Administering a proportionate response to crime because humane and good-natured social interaction, particularly when dealing with minor crime and deviance, can solve problems amicably and peacefully. As Dennis and Mallon (1998) assert:

  Whether a quality-of-life offence is dealt with by a joke, or with the lightest of hands that is required by the situation, it is dealt with a view to stopping the offence, and stopping a repetition of it.

- Policing can make a distinct difference; directly, by reducing petty crime, vandalism, graffiti and low-level disorder, and indirectly, by creating an environment that is less hospitable to more serious criminals.

ZTP is sometimes associated exclusively with a hard or military style of policing but, in fact, zero tolerance means dealing with crime or disorder at as early a stage as possible in order to prevent its escalation in areas where offending behaviour can be changed and restoring order is still possible. Moreover, Right Realists argue that resources should be employed in areas that are at high risk of becoming, or just beginning to develop into high crime areas, whereas areas where crime is already endemic should not have resources devoted to them.

ZTP was first employed as a policing strategy in New York in 1994 soon after William Bratton was appointed Chief Crime Commissioner and at a time when New York City (NYC) had a reputation as 'the crime capital of the world'.

> *Drunks and addicts could sit on the stoops, but could not lie down. People could drink on side streets, but not at the main intersection. Bottles had to be in paper bags. Talking to, bothering, or begging from people waiting at the bus stop was strictly forbidden. Persons who broke the informal rules, especially those who bothered people waiting at bus stops, were arrested for vagrancy. Noisy teenagers were told to keep quiet. (Wilson and Kelling, 1982, page 1)*

Subsequently, NYC became one of the safest big cities in the world. According to Bratton (1998), the New York City Police Department (NYPD) were principally responsible for a reduction in the city's crime rate by 37 per cent with the homicide rate alone plummeting over 50 per cent from 2,000 to 1,000 per year. Following the success of the ZTP in New York, the strategy was implemented in some UK cities.

CASE STUDY

Zero-tolerance policing in Hartlepool, UK

Crime increased significantly in Hartlepool, a town in the north east of England during the early 1990s, In April 1994, Ray Mallon was appointed as the new head of crime strategy for the Hartlepool division of Cleveland Police Constabulary. Hartlepool's crime figures were also cut. In the two years between 1994 and 1996, the total number of reported crimes fell by 27 per cent, from 15,600 to 11,300. Thefts of vehicles were down by 56 per cent, domestic burglaries were down by 31 per cent and thefts from vehicles were cut by 15 per cent. Zero-tolerance policing Hartlepool style had two aims: to reduce the number of crimes 'to the extent that this was within the scope of British policing methods' and to retain or recover the control of the streets on behalf and with the consent of the law-abiding population. In line with Broken Windows, Hartlepool police sought to achieve this by tackling anti-social behaviour and 'nuisance crime'.

Hartlepool police also used the ZTP strategy to focus on reducing repeat victim- isation; a timely decision given that from the late 1980s, the Home Office had become increasingly interested in the growing academic research in this area. The key conclusions were that a small number of offenders were responsible for a large amount of crime, a small number of targets (places or people) were suffering a large amount of crime and therefore preventing repeat victimisation was likely to prevent a large proportion of all offences. Although most repeat victimisation stud- ies are concerned with the dynamics of victimisation rather than of offenders, Pease (1998) suggests that as many as 75 per cent of all repeats could have had the same perpetrator. The Audit Commission (1993) also recommended that the police should focus on targeting offenders rather than simply responding to crimes. Based on this logic, reducing crime should, in theory, be reasonably simple because the police do not need to look very far in order to apprehend the small number of offenders who commit between 50 and 75 per cent of all crimes (especially given most of these offenders will be known to the police already). In Hartlepool, according to Dennis and Mallon (1998), the small number of burglars made the problem manageable because at any given time there were only about 30 of what Dennis and Mallon referred to as hard-core burglars. In Hartlepool, victims of crime and disorder often knew who the perpetrators were but had the perception that the police and other criminal justice agencies seemed incapable of dealing with them. Part of the ZTP strategy in Hartlepool included ensuring that offenders were identifiable to the community. Dennis and Mallon (1998, page 68) contended:

> *Simply letting the boy or the young man know that if he pushes high spirits into intimidation, if he spray paints the bus seats, if he sniffs glue under the old railway bridge, if he smashes the seat in the park, the chances have been considerably raised that someone will effectively know that he was the culprit.*

So, an element of ZTP Hartlepool style was to encourage a labelling effect upon offenders. It is usual for those who break the law to be labelled as criminal but the labelling effect can have both positive and negative effects for an offender.

Labelling effects

Labelling theorists argue that no behaviour is inherently deviant or criminal, but only comes to be considered so when others confer this label upon the act (Hopkins Burke, 2005). Howard Becker argues that society creates deviance by making the rules, which, when broken, constitute deviance, which then causes society to label those who break these rules as deviants or outsiders (Jones, 1998). Edwin Lemert developed this idea by considering two aspects of labelling: how the deviant behaviour originates (which Lemert refers to as primary deviance) and what is the influence of labelling a person as deviant on their future behaviour (which he referred to as secondary deviance).

We must distinguish here between those who commit criminal acts (that are, of course, against the law) and those who commit acts of deviance that are not. This is because illegal acts cannot be subject to the same subjective labelling as those that are not. However, what is common to all labelling is that those labelled as deviant or criminal will become stereotyped as so by wider society and second, they might eventually re-define their non-deviant self-image and come to perceive themselves as criminal or deviant (Tannenbaum, 1936). So, labelling could serve to deepen criminality and deviance, which could undermine pro-active policing strategies that rely on deterring and preventing crime and disorder. However, some have used labelling theory in a more positive respect through its capacity for re-integrative shaming.

Re-integrative shaming

Devised by John Braithwaite in 1989, re-integrative shaming is followed by gestures of re-acceptance into the community of law-abiding citizens. Whereas stigmatisation through labelling involves denigration of the person, re-integrative shaming involves denigration of the behaviour (Jones, 1998). If successful, re-integrative shaming should offer a preventative element to crime control because it should deter offenders from committing further crimes. The role of the police should also be minimal as re-integrative shaming advocates a minimalist approach for criminal law and criminal justice intervention. Some police forces began experimenting with restorative approaches to policing, particularly in relation to cautioning practices, early in the last decade.

PRACTICAL TASK

In what ways do the police contribute to re-integrating offenders into society and how might police officers be more pro-active in doing this?

Pro-active and intelligence-led policing

Pro-active policing increased in importance during the 1990s as one of the methods to improve the efficiency of the police force as part of the mangerialist agenda of the Conservative government. As we discuss towards the end of Chapter 6, managerialism refers to a variety of techniques and strategies implemented to promote a culture of cost efficiency, service effectiveness and economy – often referred to as the 3 E's. The government sought to find ways of reducing the cost of running public services including the police by making them more efficient. Part of this efficiency drive involved a government commitment to increase police numbers to try to increase foot patrols to reverse rising crime rates. The government argued that foot patrol would increase engagement between the police and the public and, under the neighbourhood policing strategy (discussed in detail in Chapter 5), patrol officers would be responsible for patrolling specific and small geographical areas, thereby enabling them to seek out criminogenic problems by means of an intelligence-led policing approach.

Intelligence-led policing

The origins of the intelligence-led policing approach are a little unclear but it seems to have emerged during the late 1980s and early 1990s as one of a number of policing strategies and approaches implemented as part of the mangerialist agenda aimed at improving the efficiency of the police force. The approach involves the police collecting information about crime and disorder problems and using a problem-orientated policing approach to analyse the information and apply reductive interventions. The police gather information from a variety of sources including:

- community residents, to whom the police talk as part of neighbourhood policing strategies (see Chapter 5);
- patrol officers;
- witnesses;

- informants;

- technology (such as CCTV).

Intelligence-led policing is driven by the National Intelligence Model which was developed by the National Criminal Intelligence Service. The model concerned with how to gather, analyse and use information collected and held by the police and provides a targeted approach to crime control, focusing upon the identification, analysis and 'management' of persistent and developing 'problems' or 'risks'. Therefore, intelligence-led policing is based upon a four-stranded approach to:

- target offenders;

- manage crime and disorder hotspots;

- investigate links between incidents;

- apply preventative measures.

The strength of intelligence-led policing as a means of collecting, storing and analysing information is in its use of technology that enables large amounts of data to be collected, stored and analysed and minute detail on written or visual data that might be invisible or not decipherable to the human eye.. Technology also enables accurate links to be made between many different pieces of information or incidents that, when considered in isolation, might not appear serious or relevant but when linked together might reveal a more serious crime and disorder problem (National Criminal Intelligence Service, 2000).

Problem-oriented policing

Devised by Herman Goldstein in the US in 1977, problem-orientated policing (POP) was introduced into the UK in 1995 and most police constabularies in the UK now purport to use it in some form (Read and Tilley, 2000). POP works by identifying the root causes of recurrent problems in a community and solving them using preventative, evidence-based, long-term strategies. Flanagan (2008, page 35) notes: *Problem solving has been a crucial part of the development of neighbourhood policing [now employed in some form by all police forces in the country – see Chapter 5 for an in-depth discussion] and there are signs that it is becoming part of the service's approach more widely*. POP fits as a strategy within the neighbourhood policing approach due to its emphasis on localised policing through Safer Neighbourhood Teams. The POP approach:

- requires the police to be pro-active rather than re-active as they look for and seek out crime and disorder problems;

- encourages *decentralisation* (whereby policing decisions are made at as local a level as possible);

- requires specific officers or policing teams to be responsible for policing specific areas, neighbourhoods or communities;

- encourages police personnel to become familiar with their area of policing responsibility and the crime and disorder problems and problem offenders therein;

- requires police officers to maintain a visible presence;

- encourages officers to look for problems and deal with them.

POP calls for close specification of problems through an analysis of the 'dynamics of offending' and deviates from the common misperception of the possibility of reducing 'crime' as a single entity. In other words, 'crime' must be analysed in the context of:

- who (the offender); does

- what (offence); to

- whom (victim);

- when (time);

- where (place);

- why (reason);

- how (method);

- what effect (possible impact of the offending).

Once problems are found, POP embraces an evidence-based approach to solving them through an analysis known as SARA:

- Scanning (clustering incidents together);

- Analysis (of the relevant offending dynamics);

- Response (action taken to address, reduce or prevent the crime or disorder problem);

- Assessment (of the first three phases – particularly the response). (Leigh et al., 1996)

PRACTICAL TASK

Explore the website of the Centre for Problem-Orientated Policing at www. popcentre.org to find out more detail of how POP is used to analyse information and help determine the most effective responses to crime and disorder problems.

One strength of POP is its use of an evidence-based approach to crime and disorder reduction as the Assessment phase requires an evaluation of the Response phase in order to ascertain whether the measures implemented to reduce crime and disorder have had the desired effect (i.e. led to a reduction in crime and disorder). If they have not, then the previous three phases should be analysed again for any errors which might have given rise to the implementation of an incorrect Response. The POP approach can be most successful when used as part of a community-orientated policing philosophy, where relations between the police and community are amicable enough for the police and public to enjoy mutual trust and respect in order that the public are prepared to confide in the police and provide them with information about crime and disorder problems in their local areas.

Community-orientated policing

Police reform and the restoration of community policing is discussed in detail in Chapter 5. Although a vague concept, community policing incorporates various strategies aimed at improving and maintaining engagement, cooperation, interaction and trust between the police and the public in order to reduce crime and disorder and improve the quality of life of local people. As we have argued earlier in this chapter, the 1980s in the UK were categorised by social and economic change, community disorder, a breakdown in trust between the police and community and, importantly, consistently high levels of crime. Although the Conservative government of the 1990s tried to implement a community-orientated policing philosophy in order to improve relations with the community and find a more effective method of policing, it was not until after the election of the New Labour government in May 1997 that community-orientated policing became the dominant policing philosophy in the UK. At the heart of the new government's law and order strategy was the commitment to deal with crime and the causes of crime, seeking to emphasise that the Right Realist, order maintenance and reactive approach to reducing crime and disorder advocated by the previous Conservative government had little impact on reducing crime or fear of crime.

Policing in a multi-agency context

The Labour government also rejected the Conservative government's reliance on the police as the sole agency responsible for the reduction of crime and disorder and advocated a multi-agency approach to reducing crime under the provisions of the Crime and Disorder Act 1998. As we explain in Chapter 5, the theoretical basis for the multi-agency approach to crime and disorder reduction is largely grounded in the sociological and psychological positivist criminological perspective (we elaborate on these perspectives in Chapter 6). The Labour government argued that reducing crime and disorder demands expertise from a range of agencies, of which the police was one, but not the only one. Under the provisions of the Police Reform Act (2002), the government also introduced PCSOs, whose role it would be to provide a visible policing presence on the streets and undertake other policing tasks that do not require the powers or experience of police officers but often take police officers away from more appropriate duties.

C H A P T E R   S U M M A R Y

This chapter has provided a valuable context for forthcoming chapters by providing a historical discussion of some of the key social, economic and political changes that have shaped policing strategy in the twentieth century. From the end of the Second World War, the police struggled to satisfy public expectations to control crime due to rising crime rates, the emergence of youth sub-culture, community conflicts and a shortage of police officers. From the late 1950s, allegations that the police were breaching their professional standards led to the establishment of a tri-partite system of governance and accountability under the provisions of the Police Act 1964, which remains as the formal basis for the system of police governance in England and Wales.

From the 1960s, governments experimented with an array of (mainly reactive) policing strategies to respond to increasing crime and disorder, of which the most popular with the government was UBP. During the 1980s, social and economic changes brought about by the policies of the Conservative government increased public discontent and policing strategies were centred on order maintenance. From the 1990s, the managerialist agenda required a more pro-active policing approach to facilitate crime prevention and early stage intervention in crime problems. Pro-active policing remained favourable into the final decade of the twentieth century when community-orientated policing emerged as the dominant policing philosophy. We will engage in a more detailed discussion of community-orientated policing in Chapter 5. The next chapter picks up on the problem of police legitimacy and public discontent with policing strategies as a starting point for understanding police culture, an area which has been subject to intensive criminological study since the 1960s.

FURTHER READING

Stanley Cohen, S (1972) *Folk Devils and Moral Panics* is a sociological study of young people and deviance and is a seminal text relating to the emergence of interactionist and labelling perspectives of crime and deviance.

Jerry Ratcliffe, J (2008) *Intelligence Led Policing* provides an in-depth account of intelligence-led policing – one of the key developments in modern policing strategies.

Robert Reiner, R (2000) *The Politics of the Police* provides useful chapters on the evolution of policing from 1829 to the twenty-first century and media representations of policing.

James Wilson, and George Kelling's (1982) *Broken Windows Thesis* provides a useful explanation of how disorderly conditions lead to deviant and criminal behaviour and how the most appropriate way to tackle criminal behaviour is by reducing disorderly conditions at the earliest possible opportunity (through a right realist criminological perspective).

REFERENCES

Audit Commission (1993) *Helping with Enquiries: Tackling Crime Effectively*. London: HMSO.

Bayley, D (2005) What do the police do? in Newburn, T (ed) *Policing Key Readings*. Collumpton: Willan.

Bratton, W (1998) Crime Is Down in New York city: Blame the Police, in Bratton, W (ed) *Zero Tolerance: Policing a Free Society*. West Sussex: Harrington Fine Arts.

Chibnall, S (1977) *Law and Order News.* London: Tavistock.

Cohen, S (1972) *Folk Devils and Moral Panics.* London: Routledge.

Dennis, N and Mallon, E (1998) Confident Policing in Hartlepool, in Bratton, W (ed) *Zero Tolerance: Policing a Free Society*. West Sussex: Harrington Fine Arts.

Flanagan, Sir R (2008) Final Report of the Independent Review of Policing.

Hicks, J and Allen, G (1999) A Century of Change: Trends in UK Statistics since 1900. *Research Paper 99/111, 21 December 1999* (Internet). Available online at www.parliament. uk (Accessed 9 February 2011).

Hopkins Burke, R (2005) *Introduction to Criminological Theory*. Collumton: Willan.

Jones, S (1998) *Criminology.* London: Butterworths.

Leigh, A, Read, T and Tilley, N (1996) Brit POP II: Problem-Oriented Policing. *Crime Detection and Prevention Series Paper 93, Police Research Group.* London: Home Office.

Mawby, R (2002) *Policing Images: Policing, Communication and Legitimacy*. Collumton: Willan.

National Criminal Intelligence Service (2000) *The National Intelligence Model*. London: National Criminal Intelligence Service.

Newburn, T (2001) Youth, Crime and Justice, in Maguire, M, Morgan, R and Reiner, R (eds) *Oxford Handbook of Criminology*. Oxford: Oxford University Press.

Orr (1998) Strathclyde's Spotlight Initiative, in Bratton, W (ed) *Zero Tolerance: Policing a Free Society*. West Sussex; Harrington Fine Arts.

Pease, K (1998) Repeat victimisation: taking stock. *Crime Detection and Prevention Series Paper 90, Police Research Group.* London: Home Office.

Rawlings, P (2002) *Policing: A Short History*. Collumton: Willan.

Read, T and Tilley, N (2000) Not Rocket Science: Problem-Solving and Crime Reduction. *Crime Reduction Research Series Paper 6.* London: Home Office.

Reiner, R (2000) *Politics of the Police*, 3rd edition. Oxford: Oxford University Press.

Reiner, R (2006) Policing and Media, in Newburn, T (ed) *Handbook of Policing*. Collumton: Willan.

Tannenbaum, F (1936) *Crime and the Community*. New York: Columbia University Press.

Waddington, PAJ and Wright, M (2010) *What is Policing?* Exeter: Learning Matters.

Weatheritt, M (1986) *Innovations in Policing*. London: Croom Helm in association with The Police Foundation.

Wilson, J and Kelling, G (1982) Fixing Broken Windows. *The Atlantic Monthly*, 249(3): 29–38.

Zimbardo, P (2007) *The Lucifer Effect. How Good People Turn Evil*. Ryder: London.

USEFUL WEBSITES

https://restorativejustice.org.uk (Restorative Justice Consortium)

https://rds.homeoffice.gov.uk/rds/bcs1.html (Home Office website of the British Crime Survey)

www.audit-commission.gov.uk (Audit Commission)

www.hmic.gov.uk (Her Majesty's Inspectorate of Constabularies – the HMIC is the independent inspectorate of the Police Service)

www.homeoffice.gov.uk (website of the Home Office)

www.popcenter.org (Centre for Problem-Orientated Policing)

LEGISLATION

Police Act 1829

Police Act 1964

4 Theories of police culture

By the end of this chapter you should be able to:

- understand a range of different theories related to police culture;
- identify the main characteristics associated with police culture;
- relate your understanding of police culture to police practice.

Introduction

This chapter provides you with an introduction to the contribution criminology has made to the study of policing during the second half of the twentieth century as well as the development of Police Studies since the beginning of the twenty-first century. The 'crisis of legitimacy' that the police experienced during the 1970s and 1980s is discussed, providing links with the next chapter on police reform. Key content includes the study of police culture since the 1960s and the impact this has had upon interpretations of the police role, the policing of black and minority ethnic (BME) communities and the role of women in policing. Further connections are provided with the contemporary diversity agenda and the complexities faced when policing vulnerable or marginalised populations.

The crisis of legitimacy

For much of the twentieth century, histories of the police in England and Wales pointed to a broad consensus that existed across society; the police were the 'thin blue line' that defended the public from offenders, danger and disorder (Reith, 1948; Critchley, 1978). But, these historical accounts of policing ignored much of the conflict that had existed since the formation of the police in the nineteenth century. The consensus myth started to fall apart during the 1960s when the rise of feminism, black civil rights and anti-war movements pointed to the different ways that the interests of powerful, establishment groups were given precedence over those who held less power.

New criminological theories were developed during this period that embodied the thinking of the times. Labelling theories pointed to the negative impact of early contact with the criminal justice system, particularly for young people, as well as the stereotypical labels that were placed upon certain types of dress, demeanour and language. Sub-cultural theories identified the importance of social and cultural identity for young people that set them aside from mainstream society and noted the concerns that this provoked from establishment institutions such as government, the media and the police. A number of Marxist theories of crime control also developed during the 1970s which focused upon the negative use of state, and therefore police, power to assert unnecessarily high levels of control over society's 'folk devils'.

CASE STUDY

What does this description from American criminologist, James Q Wilson (1968) tell you about the way police officers decide which individuals are most likely to commit offences? Can any of the criminological theories above help you explain Wilson's statement?

> *The teenager hanging out on a street corner late at night, especially one dressed in an eccentric manner, a Negro wearing a 'conk rag' (a piece of cloth tied around the head to hold flat hair being 'processed' – that is, straightened), girls in short skirts and boys in long hair parked in a flashy car talking loudly to friends on the curb, or interracial couples – all of these are seen by many police officers as persons displaying unconventional and improper behaviour. (Wilson, pages 39–40)*

The decline in police legitimacy

In Britain, the impact of these sociological and criminological developments came to the fore in the 1970s in the world of policing as increasing numbers of questions were asked about the extent of police corruption and the persistent targeting of young black males by the police (Hall et al., 1978). This period became known as the police's 'crisis of legitimacy' and is remembered most vividly in the imagery of the Brixton disorders of April 1981. Originally portrayed in the press as 'race riots', it quickly became clear that the many civil disturbances that occurred across Britain throughout the early 1980s were motivated by a rejection of the authority of the police that went beyond the issue of race. As Lord Scarman's (1982) report into the Brixton disorders made clear, inner-city communities were rejecting a culture within the police that condoned unfair targeting of minority groups and the excessive use of force.

This civil unrest highlighted the changing relationship between an increasingly diverse society and unreformed police forces. The disturbances of this period initiated a renewed focus upon the police's use of their power, discretion and position and a body of criminological literature on the subject of police culture and the use of discretion began to grow. The 'crisis of legitimacy' had been generated by decreasing public trust in a police institution that was viewed as unrepresentative, lacking transparency and being dominated by an old boys club culture that protected its own to the detriment of the broader public.

From the 1970s onwards, increasing amounts of evidence about police discrimination, malpractice and corruption became public knowledge. The West Midlands Serious Crime squad was disbanded in 1989 after a series of corruption allegations that spanned two decades. During the 1990s high-profile cases involving Cleveland Police's Ray Mallon and the Metropolitan Police's Flying Squad raised questions about the strategies used to ensure arrests. This was followed by the death of Stephen Lawrence in 1993 and the MacPherson Report (1999) into the botched investigation into Lawrence's murder. This case brought the issue of police discrimination and malpractice into the glare of the public spotlight as MacPherson declared that the Metropolitan Police were 'institutionally racist'. The central theme of the MacPherson Report was that police malpractice was not about 'rotten apples' in the barrel but that there was something wrong with police culture.

What is police culture?

There is a wide body of criminological literature on police culture. The term 'cop culture' was initially used as a shorthand way of referring to the organisational culture of the police and the working personality of the police officer (Skolnick, 1966). This culture refers to a *deeper level of basic* assumptions and beliefs *that are shared by members of an organisation* (Schein, 1985, page 6) or, more colloquially, police officer views on 'the way we do things round here'. The most widely recognised piece of work on the culture of the British Police was produced by Robert Reiner. Reiner (2010) describes police sub-culture as a complex amalgam of seven factors that are central to understanding how police officers think and interpret the world around them.

- A sense of mission.
- Suspicion.
- Isolation/solidarity.

- Conservatism.

- Machismo.

- Pragmatism.

- Racial prejudice.

Reiner's depiction of police sub-culture drew a picture of a male-dominated institution that was primarily concerned with the action-oriented side of policing *(machismo and mission)* and securing convictions *(pragmatism)* from an easily identifiable group of offenders *(suspicion)*. Viewed in this way, police officers were understood to be a tightly knit *(solidarity)* and socially *conservative* group who were prone to exhibiting signs of *racial prejudice*. The power of police sub-culture was seen to emanate from the *isolation* that police officers experienced from other members of the public through their work experience and unsociable shifts which made them more likely to socialise alongside other police officers.

Yet, while Reiner assumed that a single, monolithic culture existed within the Police Service, a multitude of subsequent studies have demonstrated the existence of a wide range of police cultures. For example, these different cultures demonstrate differences between:

- street cops and management cops (Reuss-Ianni, 1982);

- rural forces and urban forces (Garland and Chakraborti, 2007);

- male and female police officers (Westmarland, 2001; Silvestri, 2003);

- officers working in specialised departments (Innes, 2003).

Police discretion

Although a multitude of police cultures exist, their importance for criminology lies in the way in which they influence policing priorities and practice. Criminological theory has focused so closely on police culture as the *discretion* that police officers are permitted when undertaking day-to-day police work. Street-level policing often takes place away from the eyes of the general public as well as sergeants and inspectors. This renders much police work invisible and makes it difficult to monitor. Therefore, when police officers put into practice the policies and strategies devised by the Home Office and their immediate police managers they have a great deal of influence over which policies will be enforced and which will not.

Police discretion is an essential part of the police role. Police officers have the right to use legitimate force against citizens and through this they become symbolic carriers of sovereign state power. This factor alone separates police officers from the wider citizenry (Bittner, 1974; Waddington, 1999). The 2002 HMIC (Her Majesty's Inspectorate of Constabularies) report on police training noted that a police officer needs to be familiar with 5,000 pieces of legislation thus making discretion an essential part of the process through which officers decide which laws should be policed. Police officers decide when to act formally and when to act informally, who to target and who not to target and this leaves them open to accusations of over-policing and under-policing of different areas and communities. The next section introduces a wider range of policing theories and looks at their value for analysing police culture.

Analysing police culture

Much of the literature on police culture has focused upon the role of 'street cops' rather than managers, and as it is often referred to as police 'canteen' culture because of its focus on the talk that takes place when managers are absent. As a consequence of this, up until the mid-1990s the 'cop culture' literature had a tendency to focus disproportionately on the negative impact of police culture upon operational policing. These early studies focused upon police attitudes and raised questions about whether the police could provide a fair and equitable service to the public or whether they acted in a discriminatory manner that was influenced by age, ethnicity, gender, religion, sexuality or class.

Research evidence has demonstrated that cop culture exists across the globe and should thus be viewed as a product of the coercive function of policing. Despite the focus of much of the literature on Western countries, police culture is not something peculiarly European or Anglo-American. Research evidence has also shown that new police recruits have strong public service values, that they want to put something back into their community, and do not have distinct, police-focused or authoritarian personalities (Skolnick, 1966; Reiner, 1992). Adding to this, Waddington (1999, page 293) comments that the police seem to express, along with the public, *common values, beliefs and attitudes* (but) *within a police context*. Fielding's (1988) work has shown that it does not take long before new recruits start to lose their public service focus and replace it with a disproportionate preoccupation with crime control.

So, why does this cultural shift take place?

'Cop' or 'canteen' culture is based upon a premise that police work is primarily concerned with the action-oriented pursuit of offenders. Viewed from this perspective, only the police have the professional knowledge to combat the threats posed by offending communities as the broader public and their police managers do not come into contact with these people on a day-to-day basis. Therefore, a pragmatic focus on getting a dirty job done develops among street-level workers and a 'working personality' develops that informs an officer's interpretation of the police role.

But, as we discussed in Chapter 3, the majority of police time is not taken up with crime control and instead involves a multitude of mundane tasks that are often not even directly related to crime. As Banton (1964, page 85) acknowledged many years ago, *waiting, boredom and paperwork* are key parts of the police role, yet this mundane side of the role is displaced in the organisational culture with a focus placed instead upon the dramatic and the extraordinary.

REFLECTIVE TASK

Why do police officers focus on action-oriented activities in their storytelling? Think about your own experiences and the stories you tell other people about your life. What are the core components of a good story?

Understanding police and 'cop' culture

While the earlier research on 'cop' culture provided stereotypical images of the police from the 1970s and 1980s that could easily be found in *Life on Mars*, *Ashes to Ashes* or old episodes of *The Sweeney*, our understanding of 'cop culture' has matured and become more sophisticated. Developments in policing theories have resulted in a shift in focus away from the masculine emphasis upon 'real police work' and towards the different types of police officers that exist. This means we must return to the earlier point made about the existence of a multitude of police and 'cop' cultures.

In their analysis of 'Styles of Patrol in a Community Policing Context' (2002) in the US, Mastrofski, Willis and Snipes highlight four distinct officer types.

- *Professionals* – these police officers demonstrate ownership, knowledge and awareness, care and attentiveness, communication skills and good order maintenance.

- *Reactors* – these police officers are enforcement-oriented, reactive rather than pro-active, and selective about who they will help.

- *Tough Cops* – these police officers are cynical, authoritarian, crime fighters with few communication skills.

- *Avoiders* – these are the police officers who are reluctant to engage in any type of encounter.

In this typology, the professionals represent the ideal officers. Their behaviour was consistent with managerial aims and they were the officers who were most likely to take up management positions in the future. But, Mastrofski's study demonstrated that the professionals made up only 20 per cent of police personnel. In contrast, 40 per cent of officers were seen to behave and work in a way that was directly in contrast with the aims of the department. There is no equivalent research in the UK to this, but it raises some interesting questions about the future of policing.

REFLECTIVE TASK

Consider what you have learnt about police culture. How can police culture limit the impact of legislative reform upon police practice? Think about some relevant examples – to what extent have these reforms changed police practice?

Using policing theories to understand police practice

Although the theories highlighted above recognise a multitude of police cultures, much of the criminological research on the police is based upon an assumption that what the police say to researchers and their peers within their working environment is translated directly into action when they undertake policing tasks. Thereby, discriminatory talk in the canteen leads directly to discriminatory action. This is the view presented in the work of Reiner (1992) and is often described as the traditional, liberal critique of the police. The model follows these basic principles.

- Accepted practices, rules and principles of police conduct are applied at the street-level by officers.

- Police officers routinely target those who they regard as police property and focus upon crime fighting functions ahead of those related to order maintenance.

The problem with this perspective is that police researchers see only the 'back stage' (Goffman, 1959), canteen-based discussions that take place about policing with its emphasis upon crime fighting. They rarely see unsupervised routine police work as it is carried out on the streets, or the 'front stage', and this can lead criminological research to place too much attention on police 'talk' rather than police 'action'. The view that the police disproportionately act in an authoritarian and discriminatory manner is also contested by the substantial support that the police receive from the majority of the public, even during times of crisis (Loader and Mulcahy, 2003). This leads us to question whether the attitudes described in the earlier theories of police culture are transferred into the police's day-to-day interaction with the public.

Waddington (1999) views the language of 'cop' culture as representing a way for officers to live out the expectations of the job they applied for. Thus, the only worthwhile conversations are those related to crime fighting and action-oriented policing rather than that of the mundane reality of day-to-day work. From this perspective, cop culture is a form of expressive rhetoric and a means of maintaining the integrity of the world that police officers operate in. Therefore, the culture operates as a means of preserving the identity of street-level officers through stories about conflict with offenders and the restrictions presented by over-zealous managers.

'Cop culture' is a key part of the police officer's 'working personality' (Skolnick, 1966) and asserts the authority of their position and the dangers they face in protecting the public. Despite the mundane nature of much policing, police officers still possess a monopoly over the use of force in civil society and their culture is a manifestation of being custodians of state authority. 'War stories' emphasise the bravery needed for the role and dignify the 'dirty work' that the police do to help defend society. This emphasises the point Reiner (2010) makes about *isolation*: the public cannot understand what the police have to do because they do not see the dark underbelly of society.

Once again, this presents the police role as a tough and dirty job for 'real men', hence the demarcation between masculine and feminine policing roles. In a climate where officers are routinely punished for not following the rules set down in legislation, *solidarity* develops through a defensive understanding that only street cops know what must be done in order to 'fight crime'. So, while 'crime fighting' does not constitute a significant amount of police time, it is the key factor in understanding how police officers view their role as protectors of civil society.

Chan (1996) has developed this view further and emphasises the interpretive and creative aspects of the culture as well as the existence of a multitude of police cultures. These include senior command, middle management and rank and file police officer cultures. Chan (1996) suggests that police culture 'results from the interaction between the socio-political context of police work and various dimensions of police organisational knowledge' (page 110). This framework provides an acknowledgement of multiple police cultures, that works across departments (horizontally) and through the rank structure (vertically), from station to station, and even across shifts, and helps to explain the multiplicity of cultures in police forces at the local, national and international levels.

Policing theories in action

The proliferation of policing research and interest in policing theory was directly related to broader public concerns with social problems that could be linked to ineffective or unfair policing. While previous chapters have acknowledged the contribution that criminology has made to policing strategies, the focus of criminologists on police culture has been much more negative because of its concern with the high-profile subject of discrimination. Driven by the findings of the MacPherson Report and television documentaries such as the BBC's *The Secret Policeman* (2003) the Police Service's reform agenda has developed with considerable pace, most notably in the area of diversity. HMIC (2003) require police forces to identify and analyse data that represents six strands of diversity.

1. Race.

2. Sexual orientation.

3. Age.

4. Religion/faith.

5. Disability.

6. Gender.

This provides a guide to the areas where it is felt that police discrimination could impact upon communities as well as employees of the Police Service. The majority of criminological research on this subject has focused on gender and race but there are also smaller pockets of work in the other areas. While the categories of 'race' and 'religion' retain the highest public profile, the most common recipients of police attention are the young. The following sections provide an introduction to some of these areas. They are not given in order of importance but do provide a guide to the level of criminological interest in each area. Individual entries have not been provided for religion/faith and disability due to a comparative absence of research on these subjects. Readers should look at Brian Stout's *Equality and Diversity in Policing* (2010) for more information about these areas.

PRACTICAL TASK

Some of the best sources for understanding police culture are police officer blogs. These are primary sources of police officers' views and opinions. Have a look at the following and ask yourself whether the views presented in the blogs fit in with the picture of police culture that has been provided in this chapter.

Inspector Gadget – *http://inspectorgadget.wordpress.com/about*

PC David Copperfield – *http://coppersblog.blogspot.com*

Planet Police – *http://planetpolice.org*

Policing race and ethnicity

Society's folk devils change constantly over time and accusations of police discrimination against different minority groups has a history as long as that of the Police Service itself. From the working-class revolutionary Chartists of the mid-nineteenth century to the concern about Jewish ethnic communities that grew towards the end of the nineteenth century, British society has always moulded its concerns about social change around specific social groups. The most longstanding public concerns over the past 200 years have been linked to Irish migration as a consequence of the political conflict in Ireland but the roots of British criminological interest in the subject of discrimination comes out of the association made between young black men and street crime in the 1970s. More recently, this has been superseded by the association between young Muslim men and domestic terrorism as well as a range of lower level offences. In the criminological literature it is argued that these communities are both over-policed and under-protected as a consequence of the toxic mix of authoritarian governmental legislation, media-generated moral panics and discriminatory policing (Hall et al., 1978). The impact of this process is most evident in stop and search statistics.

In 2009, black people were seven times more likely to be stopped and searched than white people, while Asian people were more than twice as likely to be stopped and searched when compared to the white population (Home Office, 2010). This is a figure that has steadily increased since 2004–05. Although the number of white people being stopped and searched has increased by 30 per cent, the corresponding increase for black and Asian people has been 70 per cent (ibid.). The main reason for conducting these stop and searches was for possession of drugs. When using the extended powers available from the 1994 Criminal Justice and Public Order Act, black people become 16 times more likely to be stopped and searched while Asian people become six times more likely to be stopped and searched (Home Office, 2008). The introduction of searches by police conducted under the Terrorism Act 2000 have shown black people to be two and half times more likely to be stopped and searched than whites, and Asian people to be twice as likely to be stopped and searched than whites (ibid.).

The extent to which this disproportion is due to police discrimination or the avail-ability of particular suspect populations remains an area of fierce debate within criminology (Waddington, Stenson and Don, 2004). For example, the Metropolitan Police Service carried out 42 per cent of stop and searches across England and Wales in 2009 despite covering only 14 per cent of the population (Home Office, 2010). Therefore, a significant proportion of the difference in stop and search between the black and white populations can be explained once it is acknowledged that 54 per cent of the black population in England and Wales live in London (ibid.). Black and Asian populations are also younger and from poorer socio-economic areas than the white population and subsequently more likely to come into con-tact with the police (Webster, 2003).

Managing the poor and the socially excluded has been a core part of the police's business since the creation of the Metropolitan Police in 1829. The negative labelling of offenders and suspect populations means that the police concentrate much of their effort into policing a relatively small proportion of the population. The stereo-typing of offenders as 'suspect' can be translated into forms of discrimination and this is most visible when minority ethnic groups are targeted. The disproportionate targeting of minority ethnic groups starts a vicious circle as those targeted become less likely to cooperate with the police and poor police–community relations develop. A subsequent self-fulfilling prophecy ensures that the police's belief that they are targeting the right groups is fulfilled by the non-compliance of those suspected.

In his 1981 report into the Brixton disorder, Lord Scarman pointed towards the problems created by 'rotten apples' in the Police Service – rogue officers whose racial prejudice disproportionately undermined the good work of others. This view-point was challenged in 1999 by the findings of Lord MacPherson's Report into the investigation of the death of Stephen Lawrence which viewed racism as an insti-tutionalised problem that was often hidden away in police canteens, police sta-tions or within the procedures of the Metropolitan Police Service. The MacPherson Report generated significant resistance from the Police Service which interpreted MacPherson's findings as a slur on the behaviour of all of its officers. This had not been MacPherson's intention, but his definition of institutional racism had not helped clarify the point he was trying to make. MacPherson (1999, para 6.34) defined institutionalised racism as

> *the collective failure of an organisation to provide an appropriate and*
> *professional service to people because of their colour, culture or ethnic*
> *origin, which can be seen or detected in processes, attitudes, and behaviour,*
> *which amount to discrimination through unwitting prejudice, ignorance,*

thoughtlessness, and racist stereotyping, which disadvantages minority ethnic people.

This broad brush definition led many people, both within the Police Service and outside of it, to interpret MacPherson's findings in a way that was not only critical of the Metropolitan Police as an institution but also of all of its members. This re-enforced both concerns among minority groups about discriminatory targeting while also generating resistance to diversity training among disillusioned police officers.

REFLECTIVE TASK

Consider the above definition of 'institutional racism'. Is this something that you have witnessed and/or experienced before? Try to think of examples that have taken place in different institutional contexts – that is, work, school, college, university, socially.

The complexities involved in understanding the relationship between policing, race and racism rarely make it through to the mainstream media. The BBC documentary *The Secret Policeman* (2003) re-introduced images of overt racism among police officers that were much more easily consumed than the nuances of MacPherson's ideas which placed more weight on cultural and institutional dynamics within the Police Service rather than the role of rogue individuals.

The complexity of the discussion about race, ethnicity and policing is further complicated by the growing concern with Islamophobia, both across society and within the Police Service. Alexander (2008) comments that although there is a tendency to think about Islamophobia in religious terms, it is best understood as the latest manifestation of racism. This is not to deny that religion remains a key issue to understand within the context of police culture, but it is clear that discrimination surrounding current concerns about Asian gangs, terrorism and tensions with the Muslim community are more usefully situated within the criminological literature on police discrimination.

PRACTICAL TASK

The National Black Police Association was founded in 1998 and aims to 'ensure equitable service for all and for the Black and Minority Ethnic (BME) Staff' who it represents. The broader objective of NBPA is to promote good race relations and equality of opportunity both within the Police Service and across the wider community in the UK.

Visit NBPA's website to evaluate their aims and objectives.

www.nbpa.co.uk

Policing gender

Alongside racial prejudice, one of the other most widely commented on aspects of police culture is machismo. Machismo situates police work within a framework of masculine values and male ownership of policing functions and has been identified as being problematic for both female police officers as well as female victims of crime. There have been ongoing accounts concerning the failure of the police to respond to female victims of sexual offending and the blame for this has often been linked to police culture. The underlying reasons for this lie with the historical dominance of the Police Service by men and the police culture this history has produced. Female police officers did not achieve formal recognition of their equal standing in policing until the 1975 Sex Discrimination Act and Equal Pay Act came into force. The impact of this historical structure has meant that the number of female police officers was restricted until the latter part of the twentieth century.

The number of female police officers has increased significantly during the first decade of the twenty-first century yet the relatively recent nature of this development means that comparatively few female officers are still advancing to the most senior levels (Silvestri, 2003). At the launch of the 'Gender Agenda 2' in 2006 the successful increase in female police officers up to 22 per cent of total officer numbers was acknowledged while the failure to advance into senior positions was lamented. This under-representation has had a secondary impact on the experiences of victims of crime, for example, a poor understanding of the impact of domestic violence upon female victims.

The symbolic emphasis placed by police culture upon the use of force has, to varying degrees, marginalised female officers from some police roles despite research highlighting that force is relatively rarely used (Westmarland, 2001). While the British literature in this area has highlighted the structural inequalities for women that are generated by police culture some American writers have gone further. Prokos and Padavic identify a much more sinister explanation of the structural disadvantages that are built into police culture in the US. On the experience of training at the police academy, Prokos and Padavic (2002, pages 446 and 454) comment thus:

> *The explicit curriculum and the hidden curriculum at the police academy stood in stark contrast to one another. The explicit curriculum was gender neutral; the hidden curriculum was riddled with gender lessons ... hegemonic masculinity continually reappeared in the hidden curriculum, inserted by male instructors and staff via their treatment of each other and of women ... Male students learned that it is acceptable to exclude women, that women are naturally very different from men and thus can be treated differently, that denigrating and objectifying women is commonplace and expected, and that they can disregard women in authority.*

Whether marginalisation is produced by institutionalised structures or the role of individuals remains a complex issue but it can be concluded that the literature on policing gender agrees on the following four points.

1. Women are more commonly treated as outsiders than men.

2. Gender differences are exaggerated.

3. Language is used that can denigrate and objectify women.

4. Powerful women are resisted.

PRACTICAL TASK

The British Association for Women in Policing was founded in 1987 and is a national organisation that embraces women of all ranks and grades and aims to enhance the role and understanding of the needs of women who are employed by the Police Service. BAWP played a central role in launching 'The Gender Agenda' in 2001, and its successor 'The Gender Agenda 2' in 2006.

Visit BAWP's website to identify and evaluate their aims and objectives.

www.bawp.org

Policing sexuality

The prominence placed upon masculine values within police culture has also raised concerns about embedded negative attitudes held towards lesbian, gay and bisexual (LGB) communities, in particular the over-policing of sexual behaviour between men (Williams and Robinson, 2004). The experience of LGB communities, both within the police and subject to policing, was generally absent from police research until recently. In part, this was due not only because of the invisible nature of LGB communities when compared to visible minority ethnic groups or female officers but also because of the failure of the Police Service to keep statistical data on LGB data across forces and ranks. Like other minority groups, there is anecdotal evidence of LGB officers over-emphasising their relationship with the dominant police culture in order to embed themselves alongside their colleagues.

The historical proscription of homosexuality as a criminal act has generated further tensions related to the perceived deviance of the homosexual lifestyle. This has resulted in an under-policing of the LGB community and an unwillingness to report homophobic incidents to the police. Specific concerns have also been noted about the poor policing of domestic violence cases among the LGB community (Williams and Robinson, 2004). The Police Service have responded to these concerns with an intensification of efforts to promote the work of LGB officers and highlight areas of concern related to victimisation and policing in the broader LGB community.

> ### PRACTICAL TASK
>
> *The Gay Police Association (GPA) was founded in 1990 as the Lesbian and Gay Police Association and became the GPA in 2001. The organisation aims to promote better relations between the Police Service and the gay community while also working towards equal opportunities for gay employees of the Police Service.*
>
> *Visit GPA's website to evaluate their aims and objectives.*
>
> *www.gay.police.uk*

Policing youth and class

The 'problem of youth' remains difficult to define and often emerges as a manifestation of public concerns about the next younger generation coupled with moral panics about specific crimes which have been transmitted through mainstream media. It is an oft cited urban myth that young people commit more crime than adults. A considerable body of literature has documented the relationship between young people and the police (Anderson et al., 1994; Jamieson et al., 1999; McAra and McVie, 2005) as well as the disproportionate impact a poor relationship can have upon young black and Asian men (Webster, 2003).

While high visibility and accessibility make young people much more likely to be viewed as 'police property' the research has demonstrated how police interpretations of suspicious behaviour also revolve around issues of class (and/or socio-economic status) and their related cultural manifestations such as dress, language and demeanour. Concern subsequently surrounds the extent to which police discretion is used in a manner which exerts a form of moral, or social, discipline (Choongh, 1998) over multiple strands of diversity such as age, class, gender and race to create a permanent sub-group of police suspects.

Both age and social exclusion were recognised in HMIC's 2003 evaluation of diversity issues for the Police Service; yet they remain under-researched in comparison to the more visible concerns with race and gender. This omission remains a concern as young people have been increasingly targeted by the state since 1997 and are receiving harsher punishments for the offences that they have committed. Both these factors have the potential to amplify overall levels of offending (Flood-Page et al., 2000). Efforts to counteract these cultural issues have become more visible in recent years with the introduction of restorative cautioning and community justice panels that aim to divert a greater number of young people away from formal criminal justice processes. However there is already some evidence to suggest these schemes are mainly successful in more affluent areas rather than those areas where young people are most at risk.

REFLECTIVE TASK

What can labelling and sub-cultural theories teach us about the negative impact of police contact with young people and the potential for the future amplification of offending?

C H A P T E R   S U M M A R Y

The police routinely come into conflict with the most marginal groups in society, and like antagonists generally, they demean their opponents… If the police can persuade themselves that those against whom coercive authority is exercised are contemptible, no moral dilemmas are experienced – the policed section of the population 'deserve it'. (Waddington, 1999, page 301)

Police culture is a transient concept that helps criminologists to make sense of police practice. It is not something that defines all individual police officers but a way of understanding the working personality that police officers construct in order to work effectively while maintaining their personal and professional integrity as they carry out uncomfortable and sometimes morally duplicitous tasks. Policing theories provide a mechanism for understanding the police officers' world as well as their interpretation of the police role. This helps the Police Service identify areas in need of reform as well as the means by which these reforms should be enacted. The next chapter looks at this subject in more detail.

FURTHER READING

For a general overview of the literature on police culture the best starting point is Tim Newburn's *Handbook of Policing*. The chapters by Janet Foster (1st edition) and Louise Westmarland (2nd edition) in the handbook will provide you with more detail on the different theoretical ideas introduced here.

Brian Stout's (2010) *Equality and Diversity in Policing* (Exeter: Learning Matters) provides much more detail about the different diversity strands and will allow you to investigate each area in much more detail.

REFERENCES

Alexander, R (2008) *Re-thinking Gangs. London: Runnymede Trust*. Available online at http://www.runnymedetrust.org/uploads/publications/pdfs/RethinkingGangs-2008.pdf (accessed 10 May 2011).

Anderson, S, Kinsey, R, Loader, I and Smith, S (1994) *Cautionary Tales: Young People, Crime and Policing in Edinburgh*. Aldershot: Avebury.

Banton, M (1964) *The Policeman in the Community*. London: Tavistock.

Bittner, E (1974) Florence Nightingale in Pursuit of Willie Sutton, in Jacobs, H (ed) *Potential for Reform of Criminal Justice*. New York: Russell Sage.

Chakraborti, N (2007) Policing Muslim communities, in Rowe, M (ed) *Policing Beyond MacPherson.* Collumpton: Willan.

Chan, J (1996) Changing Police Culture. *British Journal of Criminology,* **36**(1): 109–34.

Choongh, S (1998) Policing the Dross: A Social Disciplinary Model of Policing. *British Journal of Criminology,* **38**(4): 623–34.

Critchley, T A (1978) *A History of Police in England and Wales,* 2nd edition. London: Constable.

Fielding, N (1988) *Joining Forces: Police Training, Socialisation and Occupational Competence.* London: Routledge.

Flood-Page, C, Campbell, S, Harrington, V and Miller, J (2000) *Youth Crime, Findings from the 1998/99 Youth Lifestyles Survey.* Home Office Research Study 209. London: Home Office.

Garland, J and Chakraborti, N (2007) Protean times: exploring the relationships between policing, community and race in rural England. *Criminology and Criminal Justice,* **7**(4): 347–65.

Goffman, E (1959/1990) *The Presentation of Self in Everyday Life.* London: Penguin.

Hall, S, Critcher, C, Jefferson, T, Clarke, J and Roberts, B (1978) *Policing the Crisis: Mugging, the State and Law and Order.* London: Macmillan.

Her Majesty's Inspectorate of Constabulary (2003) *Diversity Matters.* London: Home Office.

Home Office (2008) *Statistics on Race and the Criminal Justice System.* London: Ministry of Justice.

Home Office (2010) *Statistics on Race and the Criminal Justice System.* London: Ministry of Justice.

Hoyle, C (1998) *Negotiating Domestic Violence.* Oxford: Clarendon.

Innes, M (2003) *Investigating Murder: Detective Work and the Police Response to Criminal Homicide.* Oxford: Oxford University Press.

Jamieson, J, McIvor, G and Murray, C (1999) *Understanding Offending among Young People.* Edinburgh: HMSO.

Loader, I and Mulcahy, A (2003) *Policing and the Condition of England.* Oxford: Clarendon Press.

MacPherson, Lord (1999) *The Stephen Lawrence Inquiry.* London: Home Office.

Manning, P (1977) *Police Work.* Cambridge, MA: MIT Press.

Mastrofski, S, Willis, J and Snipes, J (2002) Styles of Patrol in a Community Policing Context, in Morash, M and Ford, J (eds) *The Move to Community Policing: Making Change Happen.* Thousand Oaks, CA: Sage.

McAra, L and McVie, S (2005) The Usual Suspects? Street-life, Young People and the Police. *Criminology and Criminal Justice*, **5**(1): 5–36.

Prokos, A and Padavic, I (2002) There Ought to be a Law Against Bitches: Masculinity Lessons in Police Training Academy. *Gender, Work and Organisation*, **9**(4): 439–59.

Reiner, R (2010) *The Politics of the Police*, 4th edition. Oxford: Oxford University Press.

Reith, C (1948) *A Short History of the British Police*. Oxford: Oxford University Press.

Reuss-Ianni, E (1982) *Two Cultures of Policing: Street Cops and Management Cops*. New Brunswick, NJ: Transaction Publishers.

Schein, E (1985) *Organisational Culture and Leadership*. San Francisco, CA: John Wiley.

Silvestri, M (2003) *Women in Charge: Policing, Gender and Leadership*. Cullompton: Willan.

Skolnick, J (1966) *Justice Without Trial: Law Enforcement in a Democratic Society*. New York: Wiley.

Waddington, P A J (1999) *Police (Canteen) Sub-culture: An Appreciation*. British Journal of *Criminology*, **39**(2): 287–309.

Waddington, P A J, Stenson, K and Don, D (2004) In Proportion: Race, and Police Stop and Search. *British Journal of Criminology*, **44**(6): 889–914.

Webster, C (2003) Race, Space and Fear: Imagined Geographies of Racism, Crime and Violence and Disorder in Northern England. *Capital and Class*, **27**(2): 95–122.

Westmarland, L (2001) *Gender and Policing: Sex, Power and Police Culture*. Cullompton: Willan.

Williams, M and Robinson, A (2004) Problems and Prospects with Policing the Lesbian, Gay and Bisexual Community in Wales. *Policing and Society*, **14**(3): 213–32.

Wilson, J Q (1968) *Varieties of Police Behaviour*. Cambridge, MA: Harvard University Press.

USEFUL WEBSITES

The Stephen Lawrence Inquiry (The 1999 MacPherson Report) – www.archive.official-documents.co.uk/document/cm42/4262/4262.htm

http://coppersblog.blogspot.com

http://inspectorgadget.wordpress.com/about

http://planetpolice.org

www.bawp.org

www.gay.police.uk

www.nbpa.co.uk

5 Police reform and the restoration of community policing

CHAPTER OBJECTIVES

By the end of this chapter you should be able to:

- understand the development of community policing in the UK;
- understand the social and political contexts for the implementation of police reforms aimed at improving community policing in practice and the work of the police;
- understand key theoretical bases that underpin the community policing philosophy;
- understand the future of community policing in the UK.

LINKS TO STANDARDS

This chapter provides opportunities for links with the following Skills for Justice, National Occupational Standards (NOS) for Policing and Law Enforcement 2008.

AA1   Promote equality and foster diversity.
AE1.1 Maintain and develop your own knowledge, skills and competence.
IB11   Contribute to resolving community issues.
CA1   Use law enforcement actions in a fair and justified way.

Introduction

Although a vague concept, community policing incorporates various strategies aimed at improving and maintaining engagement, cooperation, interaction and trust between the police and the public in order to reduce crime and disorder and improve the quality of life of local people. Community policing incorporates localised pro-active policing strategies with local accountability resting at its heart. As Sir Ronnie Flanagan (2008, page 7) commented:

> Policing ... is a public service and one that can only be effectively carried out with the support and consent of the public. Using and developing this

engagement with the public is one of the most important challenges in modern policing and it is a challenge that must be met at all levels. The public must always be the single most important aspect of policing. Not just because their protection, trust and confidence are the key outcomes that policing must achieve but, crucially, because it is only by engagement with the public that the police service can truly know where its targets and priorities should be. For most people, accountability, in practice, means how their local streets are being policed and how the police are treating them.

To this end, this chapter explores the emergence and development of community policing in Britain and argues that the Police Service has, at times, struggled to build and maintain public trust, support and consent. In Britain after the Second World War, support for the police from the public was easily gained and policing by consent easily accomplished in Britain because communities were underpinned by an ethos of collective (or mechanical; see Durkheim, 1933, page 226) solidarity. As this chapter explains, however, consent towards the police became less guaranteed following a breakdown in relations between the police and some communities during the 1950s, media reports of police officers' engagement in corrupt behaviour and malpractice during the 1960s, rising crime rates during the 1970s and social and economic difficulties and politicisation of the police during the 1980s. After discussing the impact of these difficulties upon relations between the police and public, the chapter explores the various police reforms implemented by the Conservative government during the 1990s, before providing a more detailed discussion of how community policing was more formally renewed under the policing policies of the New Labour government from 1997. Finally, the chapter offers an insight into the future of community policing under the policies of the new Coalition government, elected on 6 May 2010.

The emergence of community policing

The concept of community policing was first devised in the late 1970s by, Chief Constable of Devon and Cornwall Police Constabulary John Alderson as a means of providing an alternative and more effective method of policing (Alderson, 1979). Alderson argued that traditional authoritarian policing was proving inappropriate in a libertarian society experiencing increasing levels of crime. So, Alderson argued for a new style of policing in the UK, which should:

- contribute to liberty and equality;
- help reconcile freedom with security and to uphold the law;
- help protect human rights;
- dispel criminogenic social conditions;
- create trust in communities;
- strengthen feelings of security;

- investigate, detect and prosecute crimes;

- curb public disorder;

- facilitate free movement.

REFLECTIVE TASK

Which of these nine aims of community policing do you consider are the most important elements of a community policing philosophy and why?

At about the same time as Alderson was developing community policing as an alternative policing strategy in the UK, the Safe and Clean Neighbourhoods Programme was being piloted in 28 cities in the US state of New Jersey. This new pro-active style of policing intended to improve the quality of life for the people of New Jersey through reducing crime and disorder and providing visible policing. A key element of the programme was to encourage the police to maintain better engagement with the community by patrolling the beat on foot instead of driving around in cars. Five years after implementation of the Safe and Clean Neighbourhoods Programme, an evaluation of the project found that beat policing had little impact on reducing crime rates but those living in the neighbourhoods felt safer because of the increased visible presence of the police (Wilson and Kelling, 1982).

Fixing Broken Windows

We discussed the Broken Windows thesis in Chapters 1 and 3 as a theoretical basis for order maintenance and zero-tolerance policing but 'Fixing Broken Windows' has also come to provide a theoretical basis to underpin some of the elements of the community policing philosophy. First, foot patrols promote *reassurance* because while increasing foot patrols in New Jersey did not significantly cut crime, residents of New Jersey felt safer, tended to believe that foot patrol had an impact on reducing crime rates, and took fewer precautions to protect themselves. This latter result can, of course, be a negative one as it could be said people are *tricked into taking fewer primary or situational crime prevention measures and so increasing their risk of victimisation*. Wilson and Kelling also found that citizens in the foot patrol areas also had a more favourable opinion of the police than did those living elsewhere. This also proved beneficial to the beat officers, who *held higher morale, greater job satisfaction, and a more favourable attitude toward citizens in their neighbourhoods than did officers assigned to patrol cars* (Wilson and Kelling, 1982).

Second, the thesis supports the need to deal with low-level 'disorder', which, if left to continue, can generate further disorder and criminal behaviour. Wilson and Kelling (ibid.) found that at the community level, disorder and crime are usually inextricably linked, in a developmental sequence so if a window in a building is broken and left unrepaired, all of the other windows will soon be broken. Once there are no more windows to break, different forms of criminal behaviour might ensue (such as graffiti or arson), eventually leading to the area looking neglected, in bad repair and at risk of dereliction as inhabitants move to alternative nicer and less dilapidated areas. Hence, the aim of community policing in this context is to identify and deal with crime and disorder 'problems' at an early a stage as possible to prevent their escalation. In this respect, community policing should embrace a problem-orientated policing (POP) approach (see Chapter 3 for a detailed discussion of POP).

Third, the Broken Windows thesis provides an early but still relevant theoretical basis for community policing as a means of preventing disorderly and deviant behaviours, which, while not illegal or subject to police intervention or arrest, serve to impact negatively upon the quality of life of communities. Wilson and Kelling (ibid., page 1) observed thus:

> *Many citizens, of course, are primarily frightened by crime, especially crime involving a sudden, violent attack by a stranger. This risk is very real in many large cities. But we tend to overlook or forget another source of fear – the fear of being bothered by disorderly people. Not violent people, nor, necessarily, criminals, but disreputable or obstreperous or unpredictable people: panhandlers, drunks, addicts, rowdy teenagers, prostitutes, loiterers and the mentally disturbed.*

As will be argued later in the chapter, the Labour government, elected to power in the British general election of 1997, campaigned while in opposition for better legislation to deal with disorderly and deviant behaviours that impact upon peoples' 'quality of life' but which so far had been ignored by the Criminal Justice System agencies, including the police, owing to the fact that they were prosecutable.

Community policing in Britain: reform and social change

The period after the end of the Second World War to the late 1950s in Britain is often termed the golden age of policing when the police appeared to enjoy automatic consent from the community (Reiner, 2001). This was largely due to the contribution of the civilian police force during the war. Reiner (ibid., 49) comments that *by the 1950s, policing by consent had been achieved in Britain to the maximal degree it is ever attainable*. Attaining this consent was facilitated by a community cohesiveness based on a form of 'mechanical solidarity' (as first espoused by the French social theorist Emile Durkheim, writing at the end of the nineteenth and the beginning of the twentieth centuries). Durkheim (1933) proposed that earlier more simple forms of society comprised high levels of 'mechanical' solidarity characterised by a likeness and similarity between individuals, invariably from the same ethnic group, who held common and rigid attitudes, beliefs, consciences and morals reinforced by sacrosanct religious conviction (Durkheim, 1915). In such a homogenous, undifferentiated society, anti-social and deviant acts offend the strong cohesiveness and social conscience of the people and perform the important function of delineating the boundaries between those who wholeheartedly supported and those who transgressed societal values (Hopkins Burke and Pollock, 2004). Durkheim argued that crime is 'functional' in a mechanical society as transgressors can be easily recognised and the repressive and summary punishments used against those that transgress against the collective will function as a deterrent to other potential transgressors. The homogeneity of a *mechanical society and belief in social control for the good of the community*, served to facilitate support for the police in Britain. Reiner (2001) argues that during the 1950s, the police had become an accepted, glorified and celebrated institution. Images of the policeman as the 'peoples friend' were portrayed in the 1950s television series *The Blue Lamp* and later *Dixon of Dock Green*, both of which featured PC George Dixon, a warm, friendly and respected policeman living in and policing a cosy 'mechanical' community. Crime in Dock Green was little more than incidents of petty theft, and policing was consensual with community support (ibid.).

Community consensus to community conflict

According to Durkheim, with greater industrialisation, societies develop from 'mechanical' to 'organic' categorised by greater diversity and complexity and where groups are inevitably interdependent on each other and are now bound together by an organic solidarity that relies less on the maintenance of uniformity and similarity between individuals but more on the management of the diverse functions of different groups (Hopkins Burke and Pollock, 2004). From the late 1950s, the 'mechanical' ethos changed and, as we argued in Chapter 3, relations between the police and community declined due to the emergence of youth sub-cultures, rising crime rates, racial prejudice, recession and the labelling effect. The breakdown in social consensus, the reaction of the police to arising public disorder and discriminatory policing against growing minority ethnic communities caused a loss of support for the police, mainly among the working classes but reports of police corruption and miscarriages of justice also led to loss of middle-class support.

Conflict theory

Conflict theory is one of a range of theories that seeks to explain human behaviour in terms of the unequal nature of the socio-political structure of society (Hopkins Burke, 2005). Specifically, conflict theorists propose that society consists of numerous groups, all involved in a struggle to promote their interests. Some theorists, such as Thomas Sellin, focus on how the competing interests of different groups cause conflicts between those groups, while others, such as George Vold, focus on how some groups are labelled as criminal or deviant and are subsequently treated less fairly by social control agents. *Critical criminology* is a branch of conflict theory which encompasses a range of criminological perspectives that explain crime and deviance *specifically* within the context of specific power relations between, and oppression of, those perceived as powerless (such as the working classes, women and ethnic minorities) by the more powerful (Hopkins Burke, 2005). There are some specific derivations of Critical Theory that emphasise unequal or the unjust treatment of more specific groups, such as Marxist criminology (which focuses upon treatment of the underclass) and Feminist criminology (which focuses upon the treatment or oppression of women). However, 'critical' can refer to any group or individual thereof that might experience some form of oppression or unjust treatment.

Left Realism

Left Realists argue that oppression by the police towards the powerless, not only enforces the powerlessness of certain social groups, but also causes crime in three ways:

> *First, police harassment of minority groups causes resentment and feelings of helplessness that may actually encourage offending. Second, aggressive policing styles create a siege mentality among the residents of an area that discourages them from assisting the police in their investigations. Third, aggressive policing brutalises crime areas, which in turn leads to more crime. (Hopkins Burke, 2005, page 222)*

However, some Left Realists are critical of critical criminologists' standpoint that ethnic minority groups, particularly black people, experience unjustified and unfair stereotyping by the police. In the 1980s, Lea and Young observed that young black males commit more predatory crime than other ethnic groups. However, black males are also likely to reside in socially deprived areas, where crime is likely to be highest. In their sociological study of social housing allocation and racial inequality in the Sparkbrook area of the city of Birmingham, Rex and Moore (1967) found that ethnic minorities resided in streets that were littered with broken bricks and glass, where the litter bins overflowed, and resided in dwellings that had crumbling facades and paint peeling from the walls. In such deprived areas, fear of crime is likely to be high, public confidence in the police low and community policing is difficult to attain. Minority groups also settled in other large UK cities of Bristol, Cardiff, Liverpool, London, Manchester and Nottingham. Many Asians and black people arrived in Britain at the same time as crime rates began to rise. However, a direct link is hard to ascertain. Lambert's study of Birmingham concluded that first-generation immigrants were no more delinquent than the indigenous white population (Lambert, 1970). However, during the 1960s, offending rates were seen as differential between white and black-Caribbean males in relation to robbery, violent thefts and assault. That said, evidence suggests that the disproportionate arrest rate of young black males is partly due to racial discrimination and 'labelling' on the part of the police (who, argues Cohen (1973), play a crucial role in the labelling process) and that black people were most frequently arrested on suspicion of the type of offences that allowed scope for police discretion in stopping and searching members of the public (Reiner, 2001).

Labelling

Labelling theorists argue that no behaviour is inherently criminal or deviant but only comes to be so when others label it as such. According to Becker (1963, page 4):

Social groups create deviance by making the rules whose infraction constitutes deviance and by applying those rules to particular people and labeling them as outsiders. From this point of view, deviance is not a quality of the act the person commits, but rather a consequence of the application by others of rules and sanctions to an offender.

Edwin Lemert made a distinction between primary and secondary deviation. Primary deviation is concerned with who and the influence of those who apply a label. For example, someone labelled as deviant by the police or the courts is more likely to respond negatively to the label than if the label were applied by a less influential person or institution. Similarly, a person is more likely to accept the label as 'unintelligent' if the label were applied by their university lecturer than by someone less influential or less qualified to make that judgment, and the latter is concerned with the impact on the individual accepting the deviant label and identify themselves as deviant.

Stanley Cohen argued that those engaged in behaviour labelled as criminal or deviant become ostracised by others as 'folk devils'. During the 1960s, it was the 'delinquent youth' who were categorised as the folk devils among the public, who demanded that the police deal more sufficiently with young people.

Folk Devils and Moral Panics

Cohen first coined the term 'moral panics' in his work *Folk Devils and Moral Panics*. He describes a moral panic as a condition, episode, person or group of persons become defined by the public (usually in response to media representations of the said condition, episode, person or group) as a threat to societal values and interests (Cohen, 1973). Cohen argues that one of the most recurring types of moral panic on Britain since the Second World War has been associated with various forms of youth sub-culture for example, the Teddy Boys, Mods and Rockers, various Skinhead groups and Hells Angels. They all become associated with certain types of deviant behaviour (such as football hooliganism, drug abuse, vandalism and political demonstrations), which prompted a negative public reaction. Cohen's study was primarily the Mods and Rockers of the 1960s due to their being distinguishable as social and cultural types rather than just for their engagement in crime or deviance.

According to Cohen, *a crucial dimension for understanding the reaction to deviance of the public and agents of social control*, is the nature of the information received about the behaviour in question (1973, page 7). In Cohen's study of a conflict between Mods and Rockers, in Clacton on Easter Sunday 1964, where two groups engaged in violent confrontation leading to some beach huts being vandalised and windows being broken, the police arrested 97 people. However, Cohen found the press to be guilty of exaggerated and distorted reporting of the events, thereby amplifying the deviant image of Mods and Rockers and initiating inevitable calls from the public for more effective policing to control them. According to Cohen, the immediate response of the police was to employ arbitrary control tactics based upon hastily formulated rules designed to reduce the perceived disorder and suppress public fear.

Policing the crisis

Hall et al. (1978) drew upon Cohen's theory of labelling and media-driven public moral panics (see Chapter 3) by analysing the emergence of 'mugging' in Britain during the late 1960s. Like so many colloquial terms used to define criminal behaviour, 'mugging' was not a legal term nor was it new. Offences such as aggravated theft from the person ('aggravated' implies that the perpetrator used some form of violence in the course of the theft) and robbery had been in existence for many years. However, when an edition of the *Daily Mirror* reported on 17 August 1972 that *mugging, a frightening new strain of crime* (Hall et al., 1978, page 3) had hit the UK from the US, there emerged a 'moral panic' among the public about this 'new' form of violent crime, even though crime statistics did not support the public or media perception that offences against the person, which had since become known as 'mugging', had increased. As such, this 'irrational' public fear is often a common feature of moral panic but the police are forced to respond strategically in order to reduce community fear. In Brixton and other cities such as Birmingham, the police established specialist units, which were seen as a 'police force within a police force' in many areas where black people resided. Hall et al. (ibid.) argued that 'muggings' most commonly occurred in geographical areas that were highly populated by young black males and which were already associated with high levels of crime and over-policing in these areas caused the 'labelling' of black people as 'muggers and 'criminals'. In this respect, Hall et al. (ibid.) were interested in two aspects of the application of this label upon young black males; First, the impact of the label on young black males themselves, and second, the subsequent reaction of the police towards young black males. The reaction of the police was to pursue an intense mobilisation by targeting urban trouble spots and likely offenders, thereby concentrating their mobilisation in typical 'black' areas against young black males and in so doing caused deterioration in relations between the police and black community whereby each were mutually suspicious and hostile toward each other. There is also evidence that the treatment of young black people by the police was different to that administered to white youths. During questioning at a Crown Court trial of two suspected muggers, a Detective Sergeant admitted *police were on the lookout for coloured young men and when found them, treated them differently than they would, had they been white* (ibid., page 44).

Crime control from this 'Critical' criminological approach developed from the broader range of Marxist-derived 'Conflict' perspectives. Many of the arguments put forward by Hall (ibid.) are Marxist or Critical in nature given his concern with the oppressive and unjust treatment by the police of the underclass (so from a Marxist perspective) and a minority ethnic group (so from a Critical Perspective).

The moral panic of mugging during the 1970s and increasing public expectation of the police during that period led to an increase in the number of black people being stopped and searched by the police under the 'sus' laws in London and other cities with a large minority ethnic (particularly black) population. The perception of the black population was that this was less to do with crime control but more to do with racial prejudice of the police and resulted in hostility between minority ethnic communities and the police with riots in 1980 and 1981 in Notting Hill and Brixton, London, Handsworth, Birmingham, Toxteth, Liverpool and Chapeltown, Leeds.

CASE STUDY – BRIXTON RIOTS

On the night of 10 April two police officers were attempting to help a black youth who was bleeding from a suspected stab wound when they were approached by a hostile crowd. The local community was already aggravated by 'Operation Swamp' – during which large numbers of black youths were stopped and searched under the so called 'sus' laws and the confrontation quickly escalated. Over the weekend of 10–12 April 1981, over 300 people were injured, 83 premises and 23 vehicles were damaged during the disturbances, at an estimated cost of £7.5m. The inquiry into the riots was conducted by Lord Scarman (which is why the report is often referred to as the Scarman Report). He noted that this was the worst out-break of disorder in the UK in the twentieth century, which he said, was caused by the social and economic problems affecting Britain's inner cities, racial disad-vantage, and a loss of confidence and mistrust in the police by ethnic minority communities due to the arbitrary manner in which the police discharged their dis-cretionary stop and search powers. Scarman recommended the return to a more community-orientated policing approach in order for the police to develop better relations with ethnic minority communities.

In response to Scarman's concerns about the police misusing their discretionary stop and search powers, the government implemented the Police and Criminal Evidence Act 1984 (PACE). Code A deals with the exercise by police officers of statutory powers to stop and search a person without first making an arrest. In particular, Code A demands that before stopping and searching a suspect, the police must have reasonable grounds for suspicion that the suspect is carrying on their person an illegal item (such as drugs) or any item that has been, could be, or is about to be used in the commission of a criminal offence. Although Code A does not offer a specific definition of 'reasonable suspicion', it is made clear in Code A that reasonable grounds for suspicion can never be made out on the basis of personal factors alone. So, a person's race, age, hairstyle or manner of dress, or the fact that the suspect is known to have a previous conviction for possession of an unlawful article, cannot be used alone or in combination with each other as the sole basis on which to search that person. Nor may it be found on the basis of stereotyped images of certain persons or groups as being more likely to commit a crime.

Apart from implementation of the PACE, all further police reform of the 1980s was primarily aimed at law enforcement and upholding social order rather than strengthening police–community relations. However, the increase in police num-bers, in financial resources for policing, in pay for police officers and in government support for the police during the 1980s achieved little in reducing crime or fear of crime. In fact, crime rates had increased, detection rates had fallen and relations between the police and the community remained poor. The next Conservative government under the leadership of John Major sought to restore police–community relations and improve the legitimacy of the police through re-establishing the lost focus on policing by consent.

A return to community policing?

Major announced plans to implement policing policy that would be seen as more community orientated. Kenneth Baker, in his first speech as new Home Secretary stressed the importance of community policing by commenting to the Police Foundation:

> *Are the police delivering the service the community wants? Catching criminals, preventing crime, keeping the peace and restoring public confidence in the Service as a whole. Hence the importance of community policing' (Baker, 1991, page 4).*

Howard claimed that one of the greatest strengths in British policing is its local basis, which promotes decent and safe neighbourhoods through the visibility, courteousness and efficiency of the police in preventing, deterring and catching criminals.

Baker's speech also highlighted the importance of understanding and dealing with crime problems in their local context and of allowing chief constables the freedom to implement community policing strategies appropriate to the crime problems in their areas and neighbourhoods. Baker (1991, page 13) commented:

> *On my visits to local police forces I have seen the theory of local policing being put into practice. In Surrey they call it Total Geographic Policing, in the metropolitan Police they call it Sector Policing, in Thames Valley they call it Area Policing. Whatever the name, the purpose is the same; to give local officers the ownership of their patch and to give local commanders the ability to meet local needs.*

Another relative aspect of community policing namely citizen focused policing also emerged initially under the Conservative government, with Michael Howard as Home Secretary nearly two decades ago. This is concerned with ensuring the police provide a high level of service to the public. This was also the first time a government acknowledged the problem of anti-social and disorderly behaviour which, as argued previously, is not illegal nor subject to police intervention or arrest but can damage the quality of life of communities. Howard highlighted the 75 per cent of police work that did not involve reducing or preventing criminal behaviour but other disorderly behaviours. Howard also included such tasks as: domestic disputes, rescuing stray animals, traffic work, patrolling our streets, giving advice and directions or helping the lost child. In other words, crime statistics were no measure of police performance because only 25 per cent of police work involved dealing with crime or criminal behaviour (Baker, 1991, page 16). According to Howard, police effectiveness should be based upon:

- providing a fair and non-discriminatory service;

- treating people with sensitivity and courtesy;

- involvement of the public;

- personal commitment of officers;

- approachability of officers;

- contribution to a multi-agency approach to crime reduction. (ibid.)

As will be discussed later in the chapter, some of these elements remain at the core of the present citizen focused policing strategy but in the remaining years of the Conservative government, community policing was, at best, a loosely implemented idea designed to encourage the police to become more of a supportive service rather than a repressive force and consolidate a more amicable relationship with the community.

REFLECTIVE TASK

Over the last 30 years, policing styles have changed requiring the police to be both a reactive crime and disorder fighting 'force' and a softer more pro-active community-orientated 'service'.

Consider the advantages and disadvantages of pro-active and reactive policing.

The Labour government elected in the general election of 1997 aimed to put a community-orientated policing philosophy more at the heart of its policing and law and order policies. New Labour first set out its policing proposals in 1994 in the document *Policing for a New Century: A Blueprint for Reform*, which aimed to address:

- persistently high crime rates;

- public fear of crime;

- low detection (and also conviction) rates;

- variable standards of performance;

- maintaining the public's confidence in policing;

- improving visibility and accessibility in communities. (HMSO, 2001)

New Labour and Third Way community policing

The community policing philosophy seeks to employ an evidence-based problem-solving approach to understanding and rectifying the underlying causes of crime and supports three key elements of Third Way ideology: a belief in the value of *community*, and an emphasis on *responsibility* and *accountability* in two ways. First, improving engagement between the police and community thereby promoting visibility, public confidence in the police, legitimacy and accountability of the police with the public, and second, promoting 'active citizenship' and personal responsibility by encouraging the community to engage with the police and take responsibility for reporting and providing evidence of crime and disorder problems to the police.

The community policing philosophy was manifested in three key community policing strategies: reassurance policing, neighbourhood policing and citizen focused policing.

Reassurance policing

In government, most of the Labour Party's police reforms were grounded in reassurance policing. The National Reassurance Policing Programme (NRPP) was trialled in England between 2002 and 2005 and was designed to improve active engagement of the police with communities, neighbourhood security (Innes, 2010) and public confidence in the police (Home Office, 2006). The reassurance approach was based on targeting 'signal crimes', as identified by local communities as the most troublesome behaviours which have the most significant negative impact in local communities (Innes, 2010). The NRPP coincided with the implementation of the Police Reform Act 2002, which introduced police community support officers (PCSOs) who would perform the reassurance policing function. An evaluation of the NRPP conducted by the Home Office in 2006 reported improvements in public perceptions of crime rates, confidence in the police, police engagement with the community, reducing fear of crime and feelings of insecurity. Despite this, by 2006, reassurance policing had somewhat disappeared as a distinct policing strategy and integrated within a new form of community policing strategy – neighbourhood policing.

Neighbourhood policing

The National Neighbourhood Policing Programme, rolled out from 2005, aimed to provide people who live or work in a neighbourhood with the following.

- *Access* whereby local people must have regular access to a local and familiar police representative (officer, PCSO or special constable), who remains on patrol in the local area long enough to build relationships and trust with those in the communities they serve.

- *Influence* whereby local people must have genuine influence over policing priorities. The police must understand the needs and views of the communities they serve as local people are closest to the crime and disorder problems that affect local communities (Rowe, 2008).

- *Interventions* whereby the police must work in partnership with other agencies to implement interventions and solutions to crime problems. Community policing involves contributions from other agencies which might be better equipped than the police to implement interventions.

- *Answers* whereby people should expect sustainable solutions and be provided with information about who is responsible for providing the answers and implementing solutions. The police should provide regular feedback to them on what is being done. National Policing Improvement Agency (2010).

Although neighbourhood policing is a national strategy, its implementation must be highly localised to reflect the highly localised nature of crime and disorder problems. Every neighbourhood is different – and so are the crime and disorder problems faced by those who live there. So, as neighbourhood policing teams, police officers, PCSOs and special constables are responsible for policing small geographic areas to provide visibility and accessibility and seek out crime and disorder problems. Since the implementation of the Crime and Disorder Act 1998, other agencies, such as local authorities, have been responsible for working in partnership with the police as part of the multi-agency approach to crime and disorder reduction as many effective interventions demand resources, experience and expertise that are beyond the responsibility and expertise of policing agents.

Neighbourhood policing teams and the PCSOs

All police forces now have neighbourhood policing teams and the majority of foot patrols in neighbourhoods are conducted by PCSOs and special constables, who, by working in a specific targeted patrol area, are able to become familiar with that area, its inhabitants and, importantly, its crime problems. Therefore, PCSOs are central the first phase (Scanning) of the problem-orientated policing strategy (see Chapter 3 for a more detailed discussion of the problem-orientated policing strategy) as most of their time is spent on foot patrol at the heart of the community. By 2005, PCSOs had become an established part of the Police Service With a responsibility for:

> *contributing to the policing of neighbourhoods, primarily through highly visible patrol with the purpose of reassuring the public, increasing orderliness in public places and being accessible to communities and partner agencies working at local level. The emphasis of this role, and the powers required to fulfil it, will vary from neighbourhood to neighbourhood and force to force.*
>
> (ACPO, 2005)

PRACTICAL TASK

This section has provided some general detail about the neighbourhood policing strategy and explained that implementation of neighbourhood policing strategies must be highly localised to reflect the highly localised nature of crime and disorder problems.

Have a look at some police constabulary websites and reflect on:

- *how local policing areas are divided into smaller neighbourhoods that can be policed by neighbourhood policing teams;*

- *what approaches police constabularies are using in order to implement neighbourhood policing and what type of crime or disorder related problems have these approaches been employed to deal with.*

(Most police constabulary websites are in the same form; for example, www.met. police.uk; www.devon-cornwall.police.uk; www.notts.police.uk)

Citizen focused policing

Citizen focused policing is the most recent concept of the neighbourhood policing strategy and aims to encourage good 'customer service' from the police toward those who contact them.

The most recent genre of citizen focused policing was implemented in 2006 and follows the model of the private sector, where successful businesses are those with a true customer service approach (Flanagan, 2008). As such, the Police Service now also has had a quality of service commitment, which aims to encourage staff to:

- listen to and understand the needs of the customer;

- understand the needs of the customer and how they might be feeling at the time of the call;

- explain what the police can do about the matter and ensure they do what they say they are going to do;

- communicate with the 'customer' to ascertain what the police could do to seek to solve the problem that caused the 'customer' to contact the police in the first place;

- keep 'customers' up to date with the inquiry and work with them to ascertain the best way to do so.

The overall aim of citizen focused policing is to ensure the public feels satisfied with the service they receive from their local police.

The Coalition government and police reform

Accountability of the Police Service with local communities remains an important element of the policing policies of the new Coalition government, which is continuing to pursue the reassurance and neighbourhood policing roles of the police. Future police reform will focus on improving the availability and accessibility of police officers and decentralising decision making by making the police more accountable to local people, primarily through replacing local police authorities with police and crime commissioners for each police constabulary area. The government argues that Police and crime commissioners are more accountable than police authorities as they will be elected by the public, who can, therefore, dismiss their commissioner if, for example, crime and anti-social behaviour reduction targets are missed. Commissioners will also hold chief constables to account although chief constables will retain operational control of policing within their force. Elections of Police and crime commissioners are due to take place in May 2012 in every police force area. The government also hopes that Police and Crime Panels and Neighbourhood Beat Meetings will improve accountability between the public and police but as yet details of these new initiatives have not yet been announced. The government will also 'oblige' the police to publish detailed local crime data statistics every month, so the public can get proper information about crime in their neighbourhoods and hold the police accountable for their performance (Conservatives, 2010).

CHAPTER SUMMARY

This chapter has explained the emergence of community policing in Britain as a means of providing a softer and more pro-active approach to policing than the harder and more reactive policing strategies used in Britain during the 1970s and 1980s. Although 'community policing' encompasses a range of strategies, its primary aims are to improve engagement between the police and public, provide reassurance, improve quality of service and ultimately, of course, reduce crime and disorder. The Police Service enjoyed full consent from the community until the late 1950s when reports of corruption and malpractice among police officers undermined its authority. Social and economic changes during the 1970s and Margaret Thatcher's use of the police to uphold social order during the 1980s further diminished relations between the police and public. The Conservative governments of the 1990s sought to implement a more community-orientated policing strategy but there was no government commitment to establish a formal policy-orientated community policing approach until the election of the Labour Party into government in May 1997. Implementation of the Police Reform Act 2001 provided for a variety of community policing strategies such as reassurance, neighbourhood and citizen focused policing. Under the new Coalition government, community policing could be set to move from a philosophy based solely on community engagement to a philosophy whereby the public assume a more active policing role. Whatever role 'active citizens' assume, the community policing philosophy is less effective without the engagement and support of the community and other policing agents and the next chapter explores the emergence of policing in this multi-agency context.

John Alderson's, (1979) *Policing Freedom: A Commentary on the Dilemmas of Policing in Western Democracies* provides an account of the earliest forms of community policing and so provides a good prelude to the arguments examined in this chapter.

Stanley Cohen, (1972) *Folk Devils and Moral Panics* is a sociological study of young people and deviance and is a seminal text relating to the emergence of interactionist and labelling perspectives of crime and deviance.

Stuart Hall's, (1978) *Policing the Crisis* documents policing from a Critical/Marxist theoretical perspective and provides an indication of the impact of labelling on the role and conduct of the police in the discharge of their duties.

Alderson, J (1979) *Policing Freedom: A Commentary on the Dilemmas of Policing in Western Democracies.* Plymouth: McDonald and Evans.

Association of Chief Police Officers (2005) *Neighbourhood Policing. PSCO Practitioners Guide.* Association of Chief Police Officers and the National Centre for Policing Excellence. Available online at www.safer-neighbourhoods.co.uk/about-safer-neighbourhoods/national-information-links/national-publications/PCSO%20GUIDE.pdf (accessed 6 May 2011).

Baker, K (1991) Home Secretary's Lecture to the Police Foundation, 25 June 1991. Available online at https://www.1991%20The%20Rt%Hon%20Kenneth%Baker.pdf (Accessed 23 November 2010).

Becker, H (1963) Outsider: Studies in the Sociology of Deviance. New York: Thre Free Press.

Cohen, S (1972) *Folk Devils and Moral Panics.* London: Routledge.

Conservatives 2010 Big Society Not Big Government: Building a Big Society. Available online www.conservatives.com/~/media/Files/D (accessed 23 November 2010).

Cooper, C, Anscombe, J, Avenell, J, Mclean, F, and Morris, J (2006) *A National Evaluation of Community Support Officers.* Home Office Research Study 297, Home Office Research, Development and Statistics Directorate. London: Home Office.

Dempsey, J and Forst, L (2009) *An Introduction to Policing.* Belmont, US: Wadsworth.

Durkheim, E (1915) *The Elementary Forms of the Religious Life.* London: Allen and Unwin.

Durkheim, E (1933/1893) *The Division of Labour in Society.* Glencoe: Free Press.

Emsley, C (1991) *The English Police: A Political and Social History.* Essex: Pearson Education.

Flanagan, Sir R (2008) Final Report of the Independent Review of Policing.

Hall, S, Critcher, C, Jefferson, T, Clarke, J and Roberts, B (1978) *Policing the Crisis: Mugging, the State and Law and Order.* New York: Holmes and Meier.

HM Government (2010) *Tackling Anti-Social Behaviour.* London: Communities and Local Government.

HMSO (2001) *Policing for a New Century: A Blueprint for Reform.* London: HMSO.

Home Office (2006) *Neighbourhood Policing Progress Report*, May 2006. London: Home Office. Available online at: http://www.bipsolutions.com/docstore/pdf/13509.pdf (accessed 6 May 2011).

Home Office (2010) *Policing in the 21st Century: Reconnecting Police and the People.* London: HMSO.

Hopkins Burke, R (2005) *An Introduction to Criminological Theory*, 2nd edition. Collumpton: Willan.

Hopkins Burke, R and Pollock, E (2004) A Tale of Two Anomies: Some Observations on the Contribution of (Sociological) Criminological Theory to Explaining Hate Crime Motivation. *Internet Journal of Criminology.* Available online at Internetjournalofcriminology.com (Accessed 23 November 2010).

Innes, M (2010) Whatever Happened to Reassurance Policing? *Policing: A Journal of Policy of Practice*, **4**(3): 225–32.

Lambert, R (1970) *Crime, Police and Race Relations. A Study in Birmingham.* New York: Oxford University Press.

Leigh, A, Read, T and Tilley, N (1996) Brit POP II: Problem-Oriented Policing. *Crime Detection and Prevention Series Paper 93, Police Research Group.* London: Home Office.

National Policing Improvement Agency (2010) Local Policing. Criminal Justice and Local Policing Unit, NPIA [online]. Available online at www.npia.police.uk (Accessed 28 November 2010).

Police Federation (2009) *Crime and the Economy: Research Conducted by the Police Federation of England and Wales*, May 2009. Available online at www.polfed.org/crime_ and_the_eceonomy_paper_(2) (Accessed 23 November 2010).

Rawlings, P (2002) *Policing: A Short History.* Collumpton: Willan.

Read, T and Tilley, N (2000) Not Rocket Science: Problem-Solving and Crime Reduction. *Crime Reduction Research Series Paper 6.* London: Home Office.

Reiner, R (2001) Politics of the Police. Oxford: Oxford University Press, 3rd edition.

Rowe, M (2008) *Introduction to Policing.* London: Sage.

Scarman, Lord L (1981) Report into the Inquiry of the Brixton Disorders 10–12 April 1981. London: HMSO.

Wilson, J and Kelling, G (1982) Fixing Broken Windows. *The Atlantic Monthly*, 249(3): 29–38.

VISUAL RESOURCES

The Blue Lamp DVD (available from various online retail stockists)

Dixon of Dock Green DVD (available from various online retail stockists)

(These DVDs feature PC George Dixon and will provide you with an idea of policing in the Golden Age).

USEFUL WEBSITES

www.acpo.police.uk (Association of Chief Police Officers)

https://www.npia.police.uk (National Policing Improvement Agency)

www.policecouldyou.co.uk/pcso/overview.html (Police Service website with particular reference to Police Community Support Officers)

www.theatlantic.com/magazine/archive/1982/03/broken-windows/4465/ (an online version of the Broken Windows Thesis by James Wilson and George Kelling)

www.youtube.com/watch?v=cCjZEZt3QKc and www.youtube.com/watch?v=Kte0T-nPAT4

(Two video clips from YouTube of the Brixton riots)

http://news.bbc.co.uk/onthisday/hi/dates/stories/november/25/newsid_2546000/2546233.stm

http://news.bbc.co.uk/onthisday/hi/dates/stories/april/11/newsid_2523000/2523907.stm

(Two articles (including video footage) by the BBC outlining the Brixton Riots)

LEGISLATION

Police and Criminal Evidence Act 1984

6 Policing in a multi-agency context

> ### CHAPTER OBJECTIVES
>
> By the end of this chapter you should be able to:
>
> - understand the development of the partnership approach to crime and disorder reduction in the UK;
> - appreciate the key roles of the police within the partnership approach;
> - understand the various policing agencies that contribute to the partnership approach and how they might work together to reduce crime and disorder;
> - explain the key theoretical bases that underpin the partnership approach and the role of the police within the partnership approach;
> - understand how the public can contribute to the multi-agency approach to reducing crime and disorder and how this might be advanced in the future.

> ### LINKS TO STANDARDS
>
> This chapter provides opportunities for links with the following Skills for Justice, National Occupational Standards (NOS) for Policing and Law Enforcement 2008.
>
> **AE1.1** Maintain and develop your own knowledge, skills and competence.
> **IB4** Determine the concerns and priorities of communities in relation to safety, social inclusion and the prevention and reduction of crime and anti-social behaviour.
> **IB12** Design out crime.

Introduction

According to Bayley and Shearing (1996, page 585), *future generations will look back on our era as a time when one system of policing ended and another took its place.* Since being established in 1829, the police have been perceived as the main institution responsible for reducing crime. However, from the mid-1980s, government policy documents, reports by chief constables and political party manifestos began to emphasise that government agencies (including the police) could not, by themselves, succeed in controlling crime (Garland, 1996) and there emerged a clear need for a new approach to crime and disorder reduction. The idea for a multi-agency approach to reducing crime and disorder emerged from a Home Office Report published first in 1984 and then again in a 1991 report 'Safer Communities: The Local Delivery of Crime Prevention through the Partnership Approach'. Reducing crime and disorder through multi-agency cooperation was eventually established through a legislative framework (the Crime and Disorder Act) in 1998.

This chapter will focus on the pluralisation of policing provision under the Crime and Disorder Act 1998 and particularly its impact upon the role of the police. Different theoretical explanations of the pluralisation of policing will be introduced, alongside the key governmental legislation that formally recognised this process in the UK. The first part of the chapter explains the background to the multi-agency approach to crime and disorder with particular reference to the relevant provisions of the Crime and Disorder Act 1998. The chapter then focuses more exclusively on policing within this multi-agency approach by discussing the role of PCSOs (established under the Police Reform Act 2002) and special police constables. The chapter will then discuss how the government is aiming to promote active citizenship in crime prevention before discussing the role of private security agencies, which, in the past 30 years have assumed a role in policing our neighbourhoods.

Emergence of policing in a multi-agency context

Since the implementation of the Police Act in 1829, the police were always perceived as the main if not the only agency responsible for controlling crime. However, from the mid-1950s, police numbers began to fall, crime rates began to rise, legitimacy of the police among the public began to slide, and the police were moving from being a pro-active service to a reactionary crime-fighting force. At the same time, government and criminal justice agencies were facing the consequences of the 'Nothing Works' agenda created in part by Robert Martinson's (1974) review of the effectiveness of prison rehabilitation programmes. He reviewed 231 studies of prison rehabilitative programmes and concluded that

> *with few and isolated exceptions, the rehabilitative efforts that have been reported so far have had no appreciable effect on recidivism …*
>
> (Martinson, 1974, page 25)

> *education … or psychotherapy at its best, cannot overcome, or even appreciably reduce, the powerful tendency for offenders to continue in criminal behaviour.*
>
> (Martinson, 1974, page 49)

Although Martinson later acknowledged the methodological weaknesses of his research, his findings proved influential, and from the 1980s government funding shifted from rehabilitation focused crime control to law enforcement and crime prevention. However, despite the increases in police numbers, in financial resources for policing, in pay for police officers and in government support for the police, there was no significant reduction in crime. Confidence in the police also fell and evidence emerged that the public were reluctant to report crime. The first sweep of the British Crime Survey (in 1982) found that crime was approximately four times higher than was indicated in statistics recorded by the police. Research from the Crime Prevention Unit at the British Home Office showing the ineffectiveness of the Criminal Justice System alone in dealing with crime also began to emerge and Home Office circular 8/1984 was the first of several reports to focus on the need to adopt a more preventive approach to crime. It stated thus:

> *Every individual citizen and all those agencies whose policies and practice can influence the extent of crime should make their own contribution. Preventing crime is a task for the whole community. (Home Office, 1984)*

Subsequent reports from the mid-1980s by the government, chief constables and political party manifestos emphasised that government agencies could not, by themselves, succeed in controlling crime (Garland, 1996). An independent working group later presented a report titled 'Safer Communities: The Local Delivery of Crime Prevention through the Partnership Approach' at the Home Office Standing Conference on Crime Prevention in 1991 which emphasised the need for partnership and multi-agency working in reducing crime and disorder.

REFLECTIVE TASK

Have a look back at Chapters 2 and 3 as a reminder of the reasons for the formation of the 'new police' in 1829 and of the various policing strategies adopted by the police in the twenty-first century.

Safer Communities 1991

As will be discussed later in the chapter, the Crime and Disorder Act 1998 provides a legal framework for the current multi-agency approach for crime and disorder reduction, with the provisions of the act largely rooted in the findings of the 'Safer Communities' report. The working group was chaired by James Morgan and the report in also known as 'The Morgan Report'. Beginning from the standpoint discussed previously (that successive policing polices and increasing police resources and pay had little impact on reducing crime rates), the committee underlined the need for a broader approach to crime reduction through multi-agency cooperation. It highlighted the importance of the voluntary and business sectors working as partners in reducing crime and disorder as well as recommending a greater partnership role for the Police Service, local authorities and probation service. The report also stressed the need for understanding the localised nature of crime and disorder. However, the Conservative government, under Prime Minister John Major, rejected the report's recommendations and the Police Service maintained its role as the institution responsible for crime and disorder reduction under a predominantly Right Realist agenda.

PRACTICAL TASK

Have a look at the document 'Safer Communities: The Local Delivery of Crime Prevention through the Partnership Approach' and identify the key policy recommendations made in the report that now appear as part of the provisions of the Crime and Disorder Act 1998.

'Third Way' policing

The goal of the *New* Labour project was to distance itself from the *old* by developing a more relevant political agenda and a more appropriate and realistic set of policies in order to respond to a changing world (Tierney, 2006). Increasingly, references were made to the Third Way, denoting a new political philosophy aimed at achieving a national consensus on the basis of non-ideological politics and de-polarisation of established political positions of left and right wing ideologies. New Labour's law and order policies were also manifested in a hybrid of some of the features of positivism and Left and Right Realism, acknowledging the failure of positivist attempts to reducing crime through changing the offender or their environment and Right Realist approaches to crime reduction through Broken Windows policing and imprisoning offenders. New Labour sought to explain its Third Way approach to crime control in the popular sound-bite of 'tough on crime and tough on the causes of crime'.

Left Realism and multi-agency policing

Left Realism emerged during the mid-1970s out of the writings of 'new' criminologists (Taylor, Walton and Young, 1973) who argued that academics, policy makers and government were ignoring the 'real' impact of crime in relation to its social (and other) causes and impact on victims. This led to the introduction of self-report crime surveys in order to discover the extent of this 'real' impact. By the 1980s, two strands of Left Realism had developed – a strand relating to explaining the causes of crime and a strand relating to how to control it. The proposition is that both strands must be tackled in order to strike a *balance of intervention leading to a 'comprehensive solution' to crime* (Hopkins Burke, 2005, page 224). This balanced intervention approach proved highly influential in underpinning the broader focus of New Labour's multi-agency approach to crime and disorder reduction, as has *sociological positivist* explanations of crime.

Sociological positivism and multi-agency policing

The first half of the nineteenth century saw the beginning of a rapid growth of scientific knowledge and the adoption of scientific method (rather than theological) to investigate the properties of every type of phenomenon (Jones, 1998) including

93

crime. August Comte described this era as 'positivist' (meaning scientific or based on evidence). Thus, positivism emerged during the 1870s as the dominant perspective to explain crime and criminal behaviour. The earliest form of positivism, biological positivism, espoused by Cesare Lombroso, Enrico Ferri and Rafaele Garofalo, sought to explain crime through the differences in physical appearance between criminals and non-criminals. The second phase of positivism, namely psychological positivism, emerged during the 1930s under the influence of Sigmund Freud and drew upon psychodynamic explanations of crime. The third phase, sociological positivism, emerged during the 1930s and seeks to explain crime in terms of social (rather than biological or psychological) causes and this third phase underpins the multi-agency approach to crime reduction and policing as adopted by the New Labour government from 1997. Proponents of sociological positivism recommend that once the whereabouts of existing and potential 'trouble spots' are identified, these must be treated or controlled and prevented in future (Hopkins Burke, 2005, page 91).

PRACTICAL TASK

This section has offered a brief overview of positivist (biological, psychological and sociological) approaches to explaining crime and criminal behaviour. Consider the strengths and weaknesses of each approach.

The multi-agency approach to reducing crime and disorder demands that all agencies, including the police, first of all understand the social causes of crime and then work together to implement workable and evidence-based solutions (for a discussion of evidence-based policing and crime reduction see Bullock and Tilley, 2009). In order to achieve this, New Labour acknowledged that no single agency can control crime and disorder because reducing crime is difficult and requires a multitude of expert agencies working together in partnership. In particular, dealing with the social causes of crime demands an approach that extends responsibility for crime reduction beyond that of the state-funded police. As Rowe (2008, page 88) explains:

> *Even working in partnership with other agencies, the capacity of the police to improve the quality of life of disadvantaged communities is likely to remain limited. While the police might be able to take some steps to tackle causal factors [of criminal and disorderly behaviour], it seems unlikely that the police service will have the capacity to address structural problems that might generate insecurity.*

The New Labour government sought to achieve this by providing a legal framework for multi-agency and partnership working through the Crime and Disorder Act 1998.

Crime and Disorder Act 1998

The Crime and Disorder Act 1998 provides a legal framework for the current multi-agency approach for crime and disorder reduction. The act confers a statutory responsibility upon local police and local authorities to take the lead in reducing crime and disorder in local areas through the establishment of Crime and Disorder Reduction Partnerships (CDRPs) or Community Safety Partnerships (CSPs). There are two key points to recognise here. First, the establishment of CRDPs and CSPs in recognition of the fact that crime problems are complex and must by understood in a highly localised context and second, the nomination of local authorities as a 'responsible authority' in that local authorities provide or administer many of the services or interventions that can contribute to effective crime and disorder reduction strategies. The main aim of local crime and disorder reduction strategies through CDRPs or CSPs is *to reduce crime, disorder and their social and economic costs in the local authority area in a cost-effective and socially equitable way* (Crime and Disorder Act 1998).

The most relevant parts of the act to the multi-agency approach to crime and disorder reduction are as follows:

- Section 5 – creates the requirement for public bodies to work in 'partnership' (although the term partnership is not actually used in the legislation) to meet the needs of Section 6 of the act;

- Section 6 – specifies that 'responsible authorities' should formulate and implement a strategy for the reduction of crime and disorder in the area, which should be rooted in analysis of the local crime problems;

- Section 17 – provides that local authorities, and associated police authorities, to take account in all of their functions the likely consequence upon crime and disorder and to do all they reasonably can to reduce it.

Responsibilities for crime and disorder reduction under Section 17 now extend far beyond the police and local authorities and include a much wider range of agencies such as the following:

- education;
- health authorities;
- housing associations;
- private sector organisations;
- probation service;
- social services;
- voluntary sector.

Policing in a multi-agency context means that the police could be required to work with any of the above agencies depending upon the nature of the crime problem. However, the police, or other police personnel (such as PCSOs and special police constables) are often the first to recognise the need for multi-agency intervention, given their roles within the community policing philosophy and requirement to engagement with local communities as part of the neighbourhood

policing strategy (see Chapter 5 for a detailed discussion of the community policing philosophy).

Policing in a multi-agency context

As part of the neighbourhood policing strategy (outlined in Chapter 5), Safer
Neighbourhood Teams (SNTs) were established in every police constabulary area in
2004. SNTs usually consist of one sergeant, two constables (usually special police
constables) and three PCSOs who work with local people and partners to identify and tackle issues of concern in their neighbourhood. These are most likely to
be quality-of-life issues such as anti-social behaviour and criminal damage. Teams
work with local stakeholders (the public, CDRPs, local authorities and other local
organisations) to decide the policing priorities.

Police community support officers

Police community support officers (PCSOs) were established under the Police
Reform Act 2002 to perform a reassurance policing function by providing a visible policing presence in communities. Every police force employs them. Although
more renowned for their public reassurance role through their visible presence
on the streets than for their role as crime fighters as part of SNTs, PCSOs hold an
important role in SNTs through tackling anti-social behaviour and issues affecting
the quality of life of local people (e.g. by reporting vandalism or damaged street
furniture, reporting suspicious activity, providing crime prevention advice, deterring juvenile nuisance and visiting victims of crime). Like police and special police
constables, PCSOs work in a range of locations or specific areas experiencing a
particular crime or disorder problem. Although they have radios and access to all
appropriate police information systems, they do not enjoy the same powers as full-
time police officers and special constables. However, all PCSOs have the following
powers:

- issuing of fixed penalty notices (e.g. riding on footpath, dog fouling, litter);

- power to demand the name and address of a person acting in an anti-social manner;

- power to confiscate alcohol and tobacco;

- power of entry to save life or prevent damage;

- removal of abandoned vehicles. (PCSO.com)

The effectiveness of PCSOs has been debated and the Police Foundation (2009, page 4) reports *there is no empirical evidence to show whether PCSOs reduce crime, or antisocial behaviour in the areas where they are deployed*. However, in 2006, the Home Office conducted the first evaluation of the role, function and effectiveness of PCSOs and found that: *85 per cent of police forces considered that providing a visible presence on the streets was the most important role of PCSOs*. Interacting with the community and dealing with anti-social behaviour/low-level crime were considered to be the next most important functions (Cooper, 2006). However, some forces were not using PCSOs to provide a visible presence at all but to support police officers in day-to-day tasks. PCSOs do seem to have taken over community patrol duties uniformed police officers with most PCSOs spending a minimum of 50 per cent of their time on the beat in their local areas compared to uniformed police officers who spent a maximum of 37 per cent on the beat. However, neighbourhood police officers did spend most of their time dealing with neighbourhood 'incidents'.

So, shifting the responsibility for beat policing away from full-time paid police officers appears to have been a successful move because, in addition to these positive research findings, police officers can employ their more extensive powers and responsibilities in fulfilling other policing duties. However, there is an underlying assumption that PCSOs and special constables are only fulfilling a duty that police officers do not want to do anyway. As far back as 1982, Wilson and Kelling reported in 'Fixing Broken Windows' that police in New Jersey were reluctant to conduct foot patrol as it was hard work and kept them outside on cold, rainy nights (Wilson and Kelling, 1982) and others (e.g. Rowe, 2008) have documented that other research evidence suggests that police officers do not tend to rate the role of foot patrols very highly, consider it as low status work or do not perceive it as 'real' police work.

Cooper (2006) found that police officers and PCSOs recognised the importance of each of these three functions in addition to the importance of approachability, which they found was vital to members of the community for passing on information to them and for building relations with the public. Many PCSOs are also encouraged to take pro-active steps to build community relations by visiting local places such as shops and schools. Some police officers also suggested that the public perceived that PCSOs were less busy than police officers and so had more time to listen to their concerns; again, vital to members of the public who wish to pass on information. Findings from Home Office research has referred to PCSOs' offender intelligence as brilliant and suggest that they often know more than the police by possessing intimate knowledge about offenders that can take months to build up, have knowledge of emerging problems and emerging trends (such as where youths are currently congregating or the location of drug dens). Police officers also acknowledged that PCSOs are the police officers 'eyes and ears' (Cooper, 2006). PCSOs spend most of their time tackling problems such as anti-social, aggressive and abusive behaviour, drinking, drug taking and intimidation. PCSOs have been criticised for their high cost and ineffective role in detecting crime but the police will refute this claiming that the role of a PCSO is one of community-based prevention and not detection. Other criticism of PCSOs have been raised: First, because they do not have the same power of arrest and detention as the police, the police are often needed to 'finish off the work of the PCSO' (i.e. by arresting then detaining suspects) and second, the recruitment of PCSOs is at the expense of recruitment to the immediate police family, which is declining.

Despite the recent cuts in public expenditure announced by the Coalition government in June 2010, grants that fund PCSOs will continue until 2012–13 (Police Oracle, 2010) despite a reduction in funding to the police. However, some police forces have warned that cuts in funding will lead to a reduction in the number of PCSOs. The Chief Constable of Lancashire Police acknowledged thus: *This is a hugely regrettable position for us as we place a great deal of importance on the role our PCSOs play in Lancashire and know that many members of the public feel the same way* (BBC News, 2010a). Unless full-time police officers are given a revised role to include a more pro-active and community-orientated policing role, reducing the number of PCSOs will have a negative impact on neighbourhood policing. Maureen Le Marinel, branch secretary of Unison warned: *Let's be clear PCSOs are value for money. They are the visible presence on our streets dealing with local crime, anti-social behaviour and gathering vital intelligence* (BBC News, 2010a).

In the event of a significant reduction of PCSOs, the government would probably seek to recruit more special constables as they are another key member of the neighbourhood policing family.

Special police constables

The Special Police Constabulary consists of volunteer police officers. Unlike PCSOs, they wear the same uniform as the police and have the same powers and responsibilities as regular police officers working alongside them in conducting foot and vehicle patrols, assisting at accidents and providing security at public events. Currently, there are more than 15,000 serving special constables in England and Wales (Policespecials.com, 2010). Their contribution to the multi-agency approach to crime reduction is seen as particularly important through their role in local Safer Neighbourhood Teams. As community volunteers, they are also said to be more representative of the community they serve in respect of their gender, ethnic background and socio-economic group than are police officers, which is seen to help engagement between the police and public.

People become special constables for a variety of reasons including:

- to give something back to the community;

- to learn new skills and gain valuable experience;

- to challenge oneself;

- to learn first-hand about the police force before committing to a full-time job there;

- to have a second chance after an unsuccessful application for a job as a regular officer.

Currently, some police forces are considering plans to require those wanting to join the police force as full-time police officers to work in a voluntary capacity as special constables for 18 months first in order to demonstrate their commitment to the service and save police money. The Metropolitan Police estimates savings of between £12,000 and £20,000 per officer in salary costs through training Specials for free (BBC, 2010b). Specials can prove very cost effective at times when reductions in public spending reduces the demand for full-time paid police employees (such as police officers and PCSOs) while the demand for police services is maintained or increases due to the (quite tenuous) links between recession and crime. The government wants to see more special constables and denotes them as a *shining example of the Big Society in action, demonstrating the role which individuals and communities have in helping to fight crime* (Home Office, 2010).

CASE STUDY– COMMUNITY POLICING IN BEXLEYHEATH

Have a look at this BBC video clip of how neighbourhood policing teams have successfully reduced crime and disorder problems in Bexleyheath:

www.bbc.co.uk/learningzone/clips/mapping-crime-broadway-shopping-centre-bexleyheath/1124.html

When you have watched it, consider your local shopping area and consider what are the main types of crime and how might you design it out?

Crime and disorder reduction through environmental design

As discussed above, from the 1960s, sociological positivist explanations emerged as the new approach to explain crime and criminal behaviour. With that, came sociologically based interventions and solutions. Environmental criminology refers to the study of where and when crime occurs. The solution to crime and disorder, according to environmental criminologists, lies in changing the environment in which crime takes place. This is known as *crime prevention through environmental design* (CPTED). Jane Jacobs (1961) was one of the first to recognise a link between the design of urban neighbourhoods and the occurrence of anti-social behaviour. She was particularly critical of post-war urban planning, which she claimed cause social disorder in neighbourhoods. In the UK, the high demand for social housing from the end of the Second World War to the 1960s led to the construction of many mass housing estates and high-rise buildings. These estates have since gained a social stigma as troublesome or criminogenic (Crawford, 2007) and the Institute for Public Policy Research has since described them as, *... some of the country's worst failures in urban planning ...* (Pearce, 2005). Oscar Newman (1972) argued that such mass housing estates promoted indefensible space including anonymous walkways, underpasses, lifts, stairwells, long dark corridors and, importantly, no personal space for which any individual takes responsibility for looking after. In the UK, Alice Coleman (1985) identified a number of design disadvantages with mass housing estates, which she also correlated with high levels of anti-social behaviour. Both Newman and Coleman advocated changing the environment of such estates in order 'design out' crime. In order to do this, police forces now employ and work with architectural liaison officers and over the past 25 years, the Home Office has implemented numerous schemes to design out crime in high crime areas of urban cities. Newburn and Morgan (1997, page 60) argue that inter agency initiatives changed the nature of pro-active crime prevention as the *focus was no longer on crime targets or crime events but on the social environments within which offenders and crime flourish*.

CASE STUDY

Have a look at the Safer Places document at:

www.communities.gov.uk/documents/planningandbuilding/pdf/147627.pdf and then consider:

- *What are the main attributes of sustainable communities?*

- *How might you 'design out' crime to make your community or neighbourhood more 'sustainable'?*

CPTED requires the police to take an active role in crime and disorder reduction solutions and work with non-criminal justice agencies or sectors, which might not traditionally be known for their interest in crime. However criminology as a specific academic field of study is a growing discipline and attracting interest from those who might not have previously been interested in knowing or finding out about crime and other transgressive behaviours. Crime prevention through environmental design requires the police to work closely with such agencies, in particular:

- geographers;
- urban planners;
- urban designers.

Consider which other individual, apart from criminologists and the police, or business sectors might be interested in finding about crime and other transgressive behaviours and what might be the nature of their interest.

Responsibilisation

Garland (1996) argues that over the past 30 years, high crime rates have become a normal social fact in most contemporary Western societies, including Britain. He also argues that *for most people, crime is no longer an aberration or an unexpected, abnormal event* (page 446). Garland's viewpoint appears reminiscent of that of Durkheim expressed almost one century ago, that crime is a normal feature of society and a society without crime is a utopian fantasy (Jones, 1998). Garland argues that crime must be managed through responsibilisation. In other words, the focus of crime management must be upon crime prevention by responsible citizens (rather than by the state), in order to reduce opportunities for criminal behaviour. This is, of course, a contentious viewpoint because it implies that responsibility for crime control is being passed to the private citizen rather than to state agencies (such as the police and other criminal justice agencies). However, Garland rejects this and argues that the responsibilisation strategy involves the state retaining its traditional penal function (through police, courts, prisons) while at the same time engaging non-state agencies and organisations in reducing and preventing crime and disorder.

Think about Garland's argument that for most people, crime is no longer an aberration or an unexpected, abnormal event *and consider:*

• *Whether you think he is correct?*

• *Why this situation might have come about?*

• *Whether the only credible response is for individuals to assume responsibility for crime prevention rather than expect state intervention?*

Responsibilisation and administrative crime prevention

Administrative criminology emerged during the early 1980s in Britain as a critique of positivist-led attempts to find the scientific causes of crime. The basis of this argument is that the crime reduction solutions that would be needed to address the causes of crime identified through positivism would be nearly impossible to implement given the sweeping social solutions, immense political will and resources that would be required. So, administrative criminologists argue that it is better (or more realistic) to concentrate on more manageable, simpler and cost-effective methods of crime control (Tierney, 2006). Administrative criminology supports Garland's notion of responsibilisation in that it places responsibility for crime upon the offender (through rational choice theory) and responsibility for its control upon the public (through situational crime prevention).

Policing public – situational crime prevention

This different method of crime control arose in the early 1980s when faith in the criminal justice system's ability to prevent crime was practically lost and controlling crime by manipulating the offenders disposition was not proving successful. In addition, the slogan 'Nothing Works' had taken hold, crime rates were rising and the ground was fertile for the formulation of new ideas, policies and practices. While researching rehabilitation in institutions in the 1970s Clarke found that the probability of a youth absconding or re-offending while resident in a probation hostel was more dependent upon the institutional regime than on personality or background factors and that the existence of opportunities for misbehaviour was most important. Situational crime prevention involves an approach to crime prevention that revolves around reducing opportunities for crime. It comprises measures directed at highly specific forms of crime that involve the management, design or manipulation of the immediate environment in systematic and permanent so as to reduce the opportunities for crime by:

- increasing the perceived *effort* of committing the crime;
- increasing the *risks* of committing the crime;
- reducing the *rewards* from committing the crime;
- removing *excuses* for committing the crime. (Clarke, 1992)

As with all situational crime prevention approaches, none of these four approaches to reducing opportunities for crime seek to finds the causes but blocks crime in practical, natural and simple ways at low social and economic cost. Administrative criminologists also see two other advantages of situational crime prevention. First, the emphasis on 'preventing' rather than 'reducing' crime suggests that, if successful, situational crime prevention will stop or reduce significantly the occurrence of crime, and second, responsibility for crime prevention rests with the individual rather than the state. One of the most commonly stated disadvantages of situational crime prevention has been crime displacement, of which five types have been recognised.

1. *Geographical* displacement – whereby crime can be from one location to another.

2. *Temporal* displacement – whereby crime can be from one time to another.

3. *Target* displacement – whereby crime can be directed away from one target to another.

4. *Tactical* displacement – whereby one method of crime can be substituted for another.

5. *Crime type* displacement – whereby one kind of crime can be substituted for another.

However, research suggests that reducing opportunities does not usually displace crime (Felson, 1998).

Responsibilisation and active citizens

During the mid- to late 2000s many government reports and legislative changes influenced the citizen focused policing agenda, particularly the *Police and Justice Act 2006*. Although crime has been falling over successive years, the government remained concerned that detection rates were too low, public's fear of crime was not falling commensurately with falling crime rates (so there existed a reassurance gap) and public confidence in the police remained too low. In order to address these problems, the Police and Justice Act aimed to promote civil renewal through the Civil Agenda that aimed to

• strengthen and empower communities;

• create more active communities;

• make the Police Service more responsive to local needs.

The Civil Agenda had, at its heart, active citizenship and the requirement of civil citizens (in other words, us) to contribute and participate (usually voluntarily) in some way to society. The Coalition government in the UK found favour with this idea.

Since winning the general election on 6 May 2010, the new Coalition government has sought to begin building the Big Society, which seeks to 'give communities more powers and encourage people to take a more active role in their community' (Conservatives, 2010). In his first speech as Prime Minister, David Cameron called on the British public to *pull together, work together and come together in the national interest* to discharge what he perceives as their civic responsibility to improve their lives and communities. The government set out how the Big Society will affect policing in the consultation document 'Policing in the 21st Century: Reconnecting Police and the People', which provides for improvements in *public engagement* (through neighbourhood activism). These principles are included in the new Police Reform and Social Responsibility Bill, which started its passage through parliament on 30 November 2010.

Neighbourhood activism

If enacted as the Police Reform and Social Responsibility Act, everyone will, in some way, be encouraged to assume some responsibility for managing crime. In particular, Neighbourhood Activism aims to improve policing and reduce crime by creating a condition of 'active' consent and new forms of cooperation between the police and public (Home Office, 2010). The government is also aiming to restore confidence in policing and encourage more public involvement in policing. This will be achieved through such means as providing the police with information about crime and disorder problems (such as through the establishment of the planned national 101 non-emergency number for reporting crime) or encourage the public to come forward as witnesses in the confidence that they will be supported.

PRACTICAL TASK

To be able to contribute to crime reduction in your area, you need to be familiar with local crime problems. 'Neighbourhood Statistics' (www.neighbourhood.statistics. gov.uk) is a government website that provides free access to a range of local area information. Use this website to have a look at the crime data for your area.

The Big Society also has the potential to facilitate a more practical form of active policing through the recruitment of more volunteers in a variety of policing roles including as special constables or by taking part in other types of joint patrols with the police. This concept of the policing public has been considered by government before when in 1993, Home Secretary Michael Howard suggested that members of neighbourhood watch schemes could patrol local streets. Although government ministers were in favour of the scheme, opponents argued it would endanger untrained citizens. Subsequently, the plan was dropped. However, it seems that the Coalition government is planning to find new ways for citizens to assist the professional police while ensuring police officers, special constables and PCSOs maintain their key neighbourhood policing role. This could mean an expansion in the number of civilian volunteer staff who support the work of the police in non-frontline roles.

Civilian police volunteers

Most police constabularies employ civilian volunteers in non-confrontational roles with the primary aim of getting local communities more closely involved with their policing, and thereby improving the service the police can offer. Volunteers are able to assist in a wide range of activities depending upon the location and needs of the *force* and local communities but most constabularies employ volunteers in the following roles.

- Press Office support.

- Role-plays for police training.

- Neighbourhood Watch support.

- Assisting at police station front counters.

- Taking part in community safety and crime prevention initiatives and leafleting crime prevention information.

- Telephoning victims of crime for feedback on the force's performance.

- Helping witnesses or victims of crime and disorder.

- Monitoring of traffic speed in response to community concerns.

- Assisting police staff in general administrative work such as typing or filing or providing more specialist support such as language skills and computer skills communication work to departments that require them.

Consider the ways in which the public might become active citizens and contribute to policing or preventing crime in their neighbourhoods.

Private policing

The final section of this chapter focuses on private policing and we have provided a more extensive discussion of the topic in Chapter 9.

Private security companies joined the policing family over 30 years ago. Although private policing encompasses a multitude of policing and security roles, all of which have been categorised by various academics in many different ways, we are concerned, in the chapter, with those private companies that supply 'police' to conduct foot patrols on our streets. And although this chapter discusses private policing as a post-modern phenomenon, private police first emerged in Britain in the 1500s when industrialisation created wealth and landowners who wished to protect themselves from the peasants, whom they denoted as petty thieves. The establishment of the 'new police' in 1829 provided Britain with a state-funded police force and private police became less necessary. However, some 200 years on, private police are once again patrolling British streets in the post-modern epoch of risk and New Right political ideology.

Risk

Beck (1992) has argued that the processes of late modernity have given rise to new forms and types of risk and a culture which is more pre-occupied with avoiding risk, which Beck (ibid.) argues has created a 'risk society'.

Mangerialism

Managerialism refers to a variety of techniques and strategies implemented to promote a culture of cost efficiency, service effectiveness and economy – often referred to as the 3 E's. Mangerialism was one of the distinct ideological commitments of the Conservative government led by Prime Minister Margaret Thatcher from 1979. Thatcher argued that many public sector services were inefficient, uneconomic and ineffective and preferred, instead, for some services to be run by the private sector, which she believed offered better value for money and better service

105

to the consumer. Although Thatcher did not believe in privatising the public police force completely, she did allow the commercialisation of policing, which permitted private companies to enter the policing market and offer some policing services.

New Right political ideology

In addition to managerialism, other policies of the New Right political ideology of Margaret Thatcher's Conservative government also influenced the growth of commercial policing companies in the UK. First, the shift towards administrative crime management placed more emphasis on situational crime prevention such as through increased surveillance. Second, the growth of mass private property promoted 'defensible space', for which individuals took more responsibility for protecting. Third, the change in social and economic conditions (particularly rising crime, recession, and high levels of unemployment and deprivation) during the 1980s and 1990s were seen to have increased the risks of crime. So, the New Right policies pursued by the Conservative governments aimed to improve the efficiency and effectiveness of policing – but not, if possible, using only state resources but by replacing dependence on state crime control with private enterprise and individual responsibility.

Private patrolling in Britain

Although private policing patrols on the streets of Britain are not particularly usual, some private policing firms are working in local neighbourhoods at a cost to local residents who pay for the protection.

The firm Community Street Wardens introduced wardens to patrol Kenilworth in Warwickshire at the end of 2010. For £10 a month, the firm offers a response unit, a mediation service and will check properties if homeowners are away (BBC News, 2010c). Residents in Darlington are already employing private security patrols from the Sparta Security firm at a cost of between £2 and £4 per week (Entwistle, 2010). A private security firm is also on patrol in one area of Southampton at a cost to local residents of £3.15 per week (Salkeld, 2009).

The main concern about residents paying for private security patrols are as follows:

- private patrols do not hold any legal policing powers (apart from those of ordinary citizens such as the power to conduct a citizens arrest);
- they will work for those who can afford it and those who cannot will go without;
- the public police ought to be undertaking this task (particularly as the public pay for this service through taxation);
- their legal accountability is unclear;
- private security may begin crowding out public policing;
- community safety is too important to be a 'commodity to be bought and sold'.

C H A P T E R   S U M M A R Y

This chapter has explained then role of the police as a partner organisation within the multi-agency approach to crime and disorder reduction. In so doing, we have discussed key governmental legislation that formally recognises the multi-agency approach to crime and disorder reduction (such as the Crime and Disorder Act 1998 and Police Reform Act 2002) and some of the main theoretical and policy developments in criminology. The chapter has outlined some of the key primary policing agencies involved in the multi-agency approach (PCSOs and special police constables) with particular reference to their roles in contributing to environmental solutions to crime. However, we must also bear in mind that the police make a valuable contribution to reducing re-offending in many other ways (such as working with the Probation Service to manage high risk and serious offenders in the community, Education Services to apprehend school truants and local health care providers to address problematic substance abuse). Since the 1980s, the focus has shifted from crime and disorder reduction to crime prevention through responsibilisation (Garland, 1996) of the citizen, which is set to be enhanced by the provisions set out in the Police Reform and Social Responsibility Bill 2010. The chapter has also introduced other policing agencies, such as those known as private police, who make a contribution to policing in our neighbourhoods and we have provided a more extensive discussion of this topic in forthcoming chapters.

FURTHER READING

Michael Rowe's (2008) *Introduction to Policing* (chapter 8) provides a neat discussion of multi-agency policing and policing in the mixed economy. Chapter 14 of Roger Hopkins Burke's *An Introduction to Criminological Theory* provides a good background to environmental criminology and associated theoretical perspectives.

Situational Crime Prevention: Successful Case Studies (1997) by Ron Clarke outlines the root of the situational/primary approach to crime prevention and the relationship between crime prevention and environmental criminology.

REFERENCES

Bayley, D and Shearing, C (1996) The Future of Policing *Law and Society Review. Law and Society Association*, 30(3): 506–606.

BBC News (2010a) Lancashire Police to Axe All 470 PSCOs. *BBC News*, 22 October 2010 (Internet). Available online at www.bbc.co.uk/news/uk-england-lancashire-11608639 (Accessed 28 February 2011).

BBC News (2010b) New Met Police Officers 'Recruited from Volunteers'. *BBC News*, 30 September 2010 (Internet). Available online at www.bbc.co.uk/news/uk-11440985 (Accessed 8 November 2010).

BBC News (2010c) Private Security Patrols Could Patrol Kenilworth. *BBC News*, 20 October 2009 (Internet). Available online at www.bbc.co.uk/news/uk-england-coventry-warwickshire-11656604 (Accessed 10 January 2011).

Beck, U (1992*) Risk Society: Towards a New Modernity*. London: Sage.

Bullock, K And Tilley, N (2009) Evidenced-based Policy and Crime Reduction. *Policing: A Journal of Policy and Practice*, November 2009, **3**(4): 381–87.

Clarke, R (1992) *Situational Crime Prevention: Successful Case Studies*. New York: Harrow and Heston.

Coleman, A (1985) *Utopia on Trial: Vision and Reality in Planned Housing*. London: Hilary Shipman.

Cooper, C, Anscombe, J, Avenell, J, Mclean, F and Morris, J (2006) A National Evaluation of Community Support Officers. *Home Office Research Study 297, Home Office Research, Development and Statistics Directorate*. London: Home Office.

Crawford, A (2007) Crime Prevention and Community Safety in Maguire, M, Morgan, R and Reiner, R (eds) *Oxford Handbook of Criminology*. Oxford: Oxford University Press.

Entwistle, J (2010) Sparta Streetsafe Expands Service to West End of Darlington. *The Northern Echo*, Tuesday, 23 February 2010.

Felson, M and Clarke, R V (1998). Opportunity Makes the Thief: Practical Theory for Crime Prevention, *Police Research Series*, Paper 98. Home Office.

Flanagan, Sir R (2008) *Final Report of the Independent Review of Policing*. (Internet). Available online at www.polfed.org/Review_of_Policing_Final_Report.pdf (Accessed 18 January 2011).

Foster, J and Hope, T (1993) Housing, Community and Crime: The Impact of the Priority Estates Project. *Home Office Research Study 131*. London: HMSO.

Garland, D (1996) The Limits of the Sovereign State. *British Journal of Criminology*, **36**(4).

Home Office, Department of Education and Science, Department of Environment, Department of Health and Social Security, and Welsh Office (1984). *Crime Prevention*, Home Office Circular 8/1984. London: Home Office.

House of Commons (2010) Written Answers to 22nd June 2010 (online). Available online at www.publications.parliament.uk/pa/cm201011/cmhansrd/cm100622/text/100622w0009.htm (Accessed 28 February 2011).

Hopkins Burke, R (2005) *An Introduction to Criminological Theory*, 2nd edition. Collumpton: Willan.

Jacobs, J (1961) *The Death and Life of Great American Cities*. New York: Ransom House.

Johnston, L (2000) *Policing Britain*. London: Longman.

Jones, S (1998) *Criminology*. London: Butterworths.

Leigh, A, Read, T and Tilley, N (1996) Brit POP II: Problem-Oriented Policing. *Crime Detection and Prevention Series Paper 93, Police Research Group*. London: Home Office.

Martinson, R (1974) What Works? – Questions and Answers about Prison Reform. *The Public Interest*, **35**: 22–54.

Morgan, R (1991) Safer Communities: The Local Delivery of Crime Prevention through the Partnership Approach. *Home Office Standing Conference on Crime Prevention*. London: HMSO.

Newman, O (1972) *Defensible Space: People and Design in the Violent City*. London: Architectural Press.

Newburn, T and Morgan, R (1997) *The Future of Policing*. Oxford: Oxford University Press.

Pearce, N (2005) Housing Will Crumble on Shaky Foundations. *Institute for Public Policy Research* (Internet). Available online at www.ippr.org.uk/articles/archive.asp?id=1267&fID=55 (Accessed 17 January 2011).

Police Oracle (2010) *Government Ring Fences PCSO Funding.* Police Oracle, Monday 13 December, 2010. Available online at www.policeoracle.com/news/Government-Ring-Fences-PCSO-Funding_28969.html.

Rawlings, P (2002) *Policing: A Short History.* Collumpton: Willan.

Reiner, R (2001) *Politics of the Police*, 3rd edition. Oxford: Oxford University Press.

Rowe, M (2008) *Introduction to Policing.* London: Sage.

Salkeld, L (2009) Neighbours Hire Their Own Police Force for £3 Per Week. *Daily Mail.* 7 August 2009.

Taylor, I, Walton, P, and Young, J (1973) The New Criminology. London: Routledge and Kegan Paul.

Taylor, I, Walton, P and Young, J (eds) (1975) *Critical Criminology.* London: Routledge and Keegan Paul.

The Police Foundation (2009) *The Briefing. Police Community Support Officers.* Series 1, Edition 4, March 2009. Available online at http://www.police-foundation.org.uk/files/POLICE0001/publications/briefings/Briefing%20PCSO%20FINAL.pdf (accessed 6 May 2011).

Tierney, J (2006) *Criminology: Theory and Context*, 2nd edition. London: Pearson.

Tilley, N and Laycock, G (2002) Working Out What to Do: Evidence-based Crime Reduction. *Crime Reduction Research Series Paper 11.* Home Office: HMSO.

USEFUL WEBSITES

https://.rds.homeoffice.gov.uk/rds (Research Development and Statistics (RDS) website, which includes a range of research and statistics relating to crime, policing, immigration, drugs, and other areas of Home Office responsibilities)

https://.rds.homeoffice.gov.uk/rds/bcs1.html (Home Office website of the British Crime Survey)

www.crimereduction.homeoffice.gov.uk (Crime reduction website of the Home Office)

www.policecouldyou.co.uk/pcso/overview.html (Police Service website with particular reference to police community support officers)

www.policespecials.com (website of the Special Police Constabulary)

www.statistics.gov.uk/hub/index.html (online gateway to UK national statistics)

www.theatlantic.com/magazine/archive/1982/03/broken-windows/4465/ (an online version of the Broken Windows Thesis by James Wilson and George Kelling)

LEGISLATION

Crime and Disorder Act 1998

Police Reform Act 2002

7 Police ethics, values and legitimacy

By the end of this chapter you should be able to:

• understand the linkages between police ethics, values and legitimacy;
• identify the main characteristics of police ethics and human rights;
• relate your understanding of police ethics to police practice.

This chapter provides opportunities for links with the following Skills for Justice, National Occupational Standards (NOS) for Policing and Law Enforcement 2008.

AA1 Promote equality and foster diversity.
AB1 Communicate effectively with people.
AE1 Maintain and develop your own knowledge, skills and competence.
CA1 Use law enforcement actions in a fair and justified way.

Introduction

This chapter looks at the relationship between ethics and policing. This relationship is often understood through a differentiation between abstract notions of ethics and the moral conduct of police officers compared with the more practical focus of operational policing. Because of this, moral and legal principles have, at times, been seen as obstacles for police officers to get over during the pursuit of more pragmatic aims. Viewed in this way, a tension is seen to exist between ethical policing and practical policing. Despite this, 'ethical', or 'value-based', policing has remained a core (if slightly unclear) objective for the Police Service since the creation of the 'new police' in 1829.

A brief review of police websites demonstrates that 'values' remain an integral part of the mission statements of most police constabularies in England and Wales. Take, for example, the following mission statement from the Metropolitan Police:

Our mission

Working together for a safer London

Our values

Working together with all our citizens, all our partners, all our colleagues:

- *We will have pride in delivering quality policing.*
- *There is no greater priority.*
- *We will build trust by listening and responding.*
- *We will respect and support each other and work as a team.*
- *We will learn from experience and find ways to be even better.*

We are one team – we all have a duty to play our part in making London safer.
(Metropolitan Police, 2010)

This statement emphasises both the importance of clear policing objectives ('our mission') as well as the value placed upon how policing is delivered. Values and ethics remain a central part of the ongoing shift towards police professionalism. The police professionalism agenda has a vision of police forces across the globe that operate with impartiality and integrity according to clear sets of rules. Yet, as we highlighted in Chapter 4, resistance to this agenda can be presented by different aspects of police culture which challenge the integration of ethical values into what is perceived to be a primarily pragmatic role.

The demands made upon personal ethics can come into direct conflict with those demanded by organisational ethics or group loyalty and place police officers in problematic situations. Imagine a situation where you witness a colleague providing assistance to a known offender in return for important information about an unresolved case. How do you weigh up the balance between the two different cases to assess the ethical worth of the decision? Is this an ethical compromise that should be avoided under all circumstances or is it a necessary, pragmatic decision? Thus, while the law, ethics and policing are by no means seen as mutually exclusive concepts, it is clear that ethical and legal principles can be viewed as obstacles by some police personnel (Neyroud and Beckley, 2001).

This chapter provides an overview of the relationship between police ethics, values and legitimacy and their importance to understanding everyday police practice. An initial discussion of policing objectives provides some context for the section on potential ethical frameworks for the Police Service and the contemporary importance of human rights and professional standards. Following on from this, the chapter focuses on the different challenges presented by personal ethics and organisational accountability. Finally, the chapter situates the earlier discussion around contemporary debates about police ethics and police reform. This provides readers with an understanding of the importance of ethics to their own individual decision making and the consequences of this for each individual and the legitimacy of the police organisation. For the purposes of this chapter, ethics are to be understood as the processes of analysis and reflection through which we think about and understand human conduct.

REFLECTIVE TASK

Before you are introduced to debates surrounding police ethics, values and legitimacy have a look at the following two questions and note down your first thoughts.

- *Why is it important for police officers to be aware of ethical issues in their day-to-day work?*

- *How does unethical police practice undermine police legitimacy?*

Policing objectives

The first book in the Policing Matters series asked the question – What is policing? This book takes this question and provides it with a slightly different criminological perspective to ask:

- What are the aims of policing?

This raises further questions about the role (what policing should achieve) and function of policing (what it actually does achieve) that were addressed in Chapter 3. Kleinig (1996) identifies the moral foundations of policing as being connected to the relationship between the individual and the state as understood through Locke's concept of the social contract. Locke (1690) pointed out that the dangers presented by a state of nature for individuals meant that they would willingly consent to the constraints presented by government in return for the protection of life, liberty and property. Thus, government, as a key constituent of Locke's civil society, enters into a consensual social contract with individuals. This social contract serves to restrict an individual's liberty in order to protect the rights of all but should not over-extend its reach. Thus, the role of policing should be to protect life, liberty and property but without extending police powers beyond that which is necessary to secure the rights of all.

The majority of this chapter addresses the role of the Police Service although, as we outline below, ethical issues are faced by a broad range of policing agencies.

In 1829, Sir Richard Mayne's initial instructions to the Metropolitan Police stated thus:

> *The primary object of an efficient police is the prevention of crime: the next that of detection and punishment of offenders if crime is committed. To these ends all the efforts of police must be directed. The protection of life and*

property, the preservation of public tranquillity, and the absence of crime,
will alone prove whether those efforts have been successful and whether the
objects for which the police were appointed have been attained.
(Metropolitan Police, 2010a, The Primary Objects of an Efficient Police)

The role of the Police Service and the broader objectives of policing retain the spirit of Mayne's ideas but the changing nature of the social world coupled with the increasingly diverse views and temperament of the social body has meant that interpretations of the purpose of policing remain contested. A quick snapshot of the past 30 years sees the Police Service focused upon order maintenance (Scarman, 1982), crime fighting (Home Office, 1993), crime reduction (Home Office, 1998) and public protection (Home Office, 2009).

Thus, we must have a clear understanding of policing objectives before we address ethical issues. The relationship between ethics and policing is further complicated by the multitude of agencies that are involved in the provision of policing services. Though the Police Service retains unique powers their monopoly over policing services has dissipated (Johnston and Shearing, 2003) and this means that the role of ethics in policing extends beyond the role and function of the public police and includes other statutory agencies as well as those from the commercial, charitable and voluntary sectors. Because of this, the initial question is broadened to:

- What are the core objectives of the Police Service, and other policing agencies, in democratic societies?

The police provide a public service, yet the potential use of force and the threat of the removal of liberty means that this is a service that many members of the public do not wish to encounter! This means that the police have to be held to account for their actions in a way that other members of the public are not, and they are frequently required to justify why they have acted in a particular way and what they expected to achieve by their chosen course of action. This places an understanding of policing objectives and ethical issues at the heart of police decision-making at both the individual and organisational levels.

REFLECTIVE TASK

Ethical dilemmas face us in all walks of life. Take, for example, a problem that affects students. You borrow a friend's laptop and find another student's essay on it. You ask them about this and the friend says that they borrowed it to help them with their essay. You subsequently find out that the other student's essay has been submitted by your friend and that they are both accusing each other of copying the original essay. What do you do?

We all face ethical dilemmas throughout the course of our lives but the role of the police in society makes this a more enduring issue for police officers. A brief review of media coverage of the Police Service introduces students to two contradictory images. One of the police as heroes and the thin blue line that protects society and another which focuses upon incompetent or inefficient policing and police misconduct. Consequently, the Police Service and individual police officers need to work with clear objectives and within a clear ethical framework which can be used to justify the often contentious and contested decisions that they make. It is this process that ensures that it is the former image that prevails.

An ethical framework for policing

A review of the criminological literature on police ethics identifies three well-known philosophical frameworks within which we can ground individual and organisational ethics of policing. A brief introduction to each area will now be provided although more detail is provided in Brian Stout's (2010) *Equality and Diversity in Policing* from the Policing Matters series.

What you do not want done to yourself, do not do to others   This ethic of reciprocity emanates out of classical philosophy and religious teachings and states that we should treat others as we would wish to be treated. While this principle provides a clear basis for individual decision making it is compromised whenever there is more than one conflicting viewpoint which must be addressed.

Kant and duty   The Kantian ethics of duty presuppose that there is a universal law of right and wrong. Kant's first general principle is that all people should be treated with respect regardless of their previous behaviour and acts. Kant's second principle insists that we have a duty to do the right thing at all times and consistently follow a code of ethics. Once again, the Kantian ethical system is too rigid to be applied directly to all of the ethical dilemmas that police officers face.

Utilitarianism   Rather than focusing on what a police officer does, utilitarianism focuses upon securing the right outcome or consequence. Thus, ethical action is measured by its utility – that which produces the greatest good for the greatest number of people. This view, most commonly associated with John Stuart Mill and Jeremy Bentham, has an ideological fit with the pragmatic concerns of police officers that we introduced at the beginning of the chapter. Unfortunately, utilitarianism can also become a justification for the excessive use of force and other forms of 'noble cause' corruption.

Having noted the incompatibility of these ethical standpoints with the varied and complex duties and tasks undertaken by police officers, Neyroud and Beckley (2001) take some of the values from these (and other) frameworks to provide a set of principles which construct a potential framework for policing.

Principles of policing

- *Respect for personal autonomy*: this is derived from the ethics of duty and in policing would include respecting the rights of citizens, showing dignity and respect for them and to colleagues and not using either as a means to an end.

- *Benificence and non-malificence* require police officers to help people without harming others.

- *Justice*, including, above all, respect for people's human rights and for morally respectable laws.

- *Responsibility*, which would require police officers to justify their actions and take personal ownership of them.

- *Care*, emphasising the interdependence of police officers and the individuals they deal with and the communities they serve.

- *Honesty*, which is a key virtue and one that is central to policing and authority and the legitimacy of individual officers.

- *Stewardship*, which emphasises the idea of trusteeship over the powerless and over police powers.

Fundamentally, ethics are about *how police officers and police leaders make the right judgements and do the right things, for the right reasons* (Neyroud and Beckley, 2001, page 37). But the principles outlined above provide a clearer framework for thinking about what ethics mean in practice. There are different philosophies of ethics which means that the Police Service in England and Wales has not yet constructed or adopted a formal code of police ethics. It may be easy to recognise unethical behaviour such as taking bribes or the excessive use of force but providing a universal definition of ethical behaviour has proved to be enduringly problematic.

Further discussion of principles in policing can be found in the Patten Report (1999), the MacPherson Report (1999) and Alderson's 'Principled Policing' (1998).

PRACTICAL TASK

The European Code of Police Ethics (2001) provides some common principles and guidelines for policing across Europe: www.coe.int/t/e/legal_affairs/legal_co-operation/police_and_internal_security/documents/Rec(2001)10_ENG4831–7.pdf. Familiarise yourself with this document and its arguments about the universality of policing objectives. Do you agree with the principles outlined in this chapter and those in the European code? To what extent do you agree with the Council of Europe's assertions about the need to progressively implement the European code in each European nation-state? No such code exists in the UK although guidelines are evident in Human Rights frameworks.

Policing and human rights

A formal framework for the protection of citizens from the abuse or misuse of state power is provided by the UN Declaration of Human Rights which increasingly influenced policing in the UK throughout the 1990s, most obviously through the introduction of the Human Rights Act 1998. The Human Rights Act 1998 made it unlawful for public authorities to act in a way that is incompatible with decisions made by the European Court of Human Rights in Strasbourg. This provided a statutory obligation to respect the following articles.

1. An obligation to respect human rights
2. The right to life
3. The prohibition of torture
4. The prohibition of slavery and forced labour
5. The right to liberty and security
6. The right to a fair trial
7. No punishment without law
8. The right to respect for private and family life
9. Freedom of thought, conscience and religion
10. Freedom of expression
11. Freedom of assembly
12. The right to marry
13. The right to effective remedy
14. The prohibition of discrimination

PRACTICAL TASK

Have a look at the following link:

www.eycb.coe.int/compass/en/pdf/6_7.pdf

which takes you to the Council of Europe's manual on human rights education and familiarise yourself with the different rights. How many of these rights do you think are applicable to policing? Are these rights similar to the principles introduced in the previous section?

The introduction of the Human Rights Act into UK law placed an emphasis on *proportionality* in police decision making, or *the need to find a fair balance between the protection of individual rights and the interests of the community at large* (Starmer, 1999, page 169). Policing in a human rights-compliant way, ethical policing and ensuring public confidence represent three ways in which the police attempt to provide a value-led approach to policing. None of these approaches is unproblematic. There are fears that a human rights approach to policing encourages 'risk-averse' responses from the Police Service (Flanagan, 2008), that ethical policing is too abstract a concept and that too much of a focus on public confidence distracts attention away from more serious offences.

CASE STUDY

An officer stops a woman who has an outstanding warrant for arrest for shoplifting. The woman has her infant child with her. Should the officer take the baby into care and the woman into custody, make arrangements for someone else to care for the baby, or just let the offender go and tell her to take care of the warrant on her own? She has no money and gives the officer no trouble.

To explore this further, ask yourself the following questions:

* *What are the ethical considerations you need to think about here?*

* *What does the law require?*

* *What do personal ethics require?*

* *What do the public want you to do?*

Values, ethics and professional standards

Having outlined what could be included in an ethical framework for policing the following sections put these ideas into practice. At the beginning of this chapter it was noted that most police constabularies have a statement of values which is linked to their strategic objectives, thus linking the *means* (or, how you do something) to the *ends* (what it achieves) of policing. Viewed in this way, values can be understood as the cumulative action of the constabulary and its commitment to ethical policing. An example of this can be provided from Thames Valley Police's statement of values:

Our aim

Working in partnership to make our community safer.

Our values

To foster the trust and confidence of our community, we will:

* *Treat everyone fairly and with respect.*

* *Act with courage and integrity.*

* *Take pride in delivering a high quality service and keeping our promises.*

* *Engage, listen, and respond.*

* *Learn from experience and always seek to improve.*

(Thames Valley Police, 2010)

A statement of values ensures that the constabulary has collective standards that must be met and provides a framework for individual officer accountability. While police accountability structures traditionally looked retrospectively at police wrong-doing, recent years bear witness to more future-oriented thinking through the development of an ethical framework for policing that aims to improve policing standards, as demonstrated in the statement above. This approach is most clearly embodied in the replacement of the (negative and retrospective) complaints and discipline system with the (positive and future-oriented) system of police professional standards.

To emphasise this point, the Independent Police Complaints Commission (2010) has provided a list of standards that are expected from all police officers:

Standards of professional behaviour

Honesty and integrity: Police officers are honest, act with integrity and do not compromise or abuse their position.

Authority, respect and courtesy: Police officers act with self-control and tolerance, treating members of the public and colleagues with respect and courtesy. Police officers do not abuse their powers or authority and respect the rights of all individuals.

Equality and diversity: Police officers act with fairness and impartiality. They do not discriminate unlawfully or unfairly.

Use of force: Police officers only use force to the extent that it is necessary, proportionate and reasonable in all the circumstances.

Orders and instructions: Police officers only give and carry out lawful orders and instructions. Police officers abide by police regulations, force policies and lawful orders.

Duties and responsibilities: Police officers are diligent in the exercise of their duties and responsibilities.

Confidentiality: Police officers treat information with respect and access or disclose it only in the proper course of police duties.

Fitness for duty: Police officers when on duty or presenting themselves for duty are fit to carry out their duties and responsibilities.

Discreditable conduct: Police officers behave in a manner which does not discredit the Police Service or undermine public confidence, whether on or off duty. Police officers report any action taken against them for a criminal offence, conditions imposed by a court or the receipt of any penalty notice.

Challenging and reporting improper conduct: Police officers report, challenge or take action against the conduct of colleagues which has fallen below the standards of professional behaviour expected.

Police work involves judgements about right and wrong, what is a crime and what is not a crime, when to use force and when not to use force, and many other things. This makes ethics and professional standards unavoidable issues for police officers. The powers that are held in the office of constable mean that it is essential for police officers to recognise the ethical issues that exist as they go about their day-to-day work.

CASE STUDY

The following short case studies look at a range of ethical problems you are likely to come across.

To explore each case study further, ask yourself the same questions as earlier:

- *What are the ethical considerations you need to think about here?*
- *What does the law require?*
- *What do personal ethics require?*
- *What do the public want you to do?*

Duty
You are returning to the station after working the late shift and notice a traffic jam. As you get nearer to the incident you realise that an accident has taken place involving a car and a bollard in the centre of the road. Do you stop and provide assistance or make your way back to the station?

Honesty
A police officer is interrogating a criminal suspect. During the interrogation the officer falsely states that an accomplice to the crime has already confessed. Is the officer's lack of truthfulness unethical? Explain.

Loyalty
While you are on your second journey in a police car your probationary officer scrapes the car along a wall as he leaves the police station. With no witnesses present the officer considers claiming that another car collided with the car elsewhere. What do you do?

Honesty versus loyalty
You are on a night out with your new shift when a colleague offers you cocaine. You question them about this but your colleague responds by saying 'don't worry, everybody does it. It's all ok with the sergeant'. What do you do?

Having decided not to say anything a turn of events brings this issue up again. Three months later your sergeant is arrested for a public order offence and accusations are made by several members of the public about a group of officers taking drugs. What do you do now?

Discretion

You stop a speeding car. It is doing 45mph in a 30mph residential zone. On approaching the car you realise that the driver of the car is an officer from your force. Do you proceed with the speeding charge?

There are no right or wrong answers to the case studies set out above. They all involve ethical dilemmas which aim to shed light on the complex nature of putting ethical policing into practice.

Personal ethics and decision making

Discretion remains central to most police work as police officers need to be seen to be acting in a fair and impartial way (HMIC, 1999). Having viewed the different tasks and case studies throughout this chapter it should be clear that ethical decision making cannot be grounded in simplistic notions of 'good' and 'bad'. Decision making often takes place in grey ethical areas that can leave officers having to explain their actions to their superiors and the wider public. This is one of the reasons policing remains such a contentious subject and the standards required of police officers remain higher than those expected of the rest of the population. A multitude of different views exist about the use of police discretion (understood here as their scope for choice) and the way in which police officers interpret and apply the law. Some people believe that police discretion should be tightly regulated while others think that police officers should be allowed to use their professional judgement to inform their decision making without cumbersome and bureaucratic regulations.

Police discretion raises four different types of issue (Kleinig, 1996):

1. *Scope* – should I intervene?

2. *Interpretation* – how should I resolve this?

3. *Prioritisation* – which crimes should we focus on?

4. *Tactics* – how should we resolve this?

None of these four areas has clear boundaries when it comes to decision making yet the consequences of making the wrong decisions are evident in high-profile cases such as the Brixton riots, the death of Stephen Lawrence and a multitude of miscarriages of justice which have left an enduring imprint upon police legitimacy. Once links have been made between ethics, values and police practice, it becomes clear that a renewed focus is needed that links ethics to decision making in order to ensure you make the right judgements in particular contexts. The desire for increased professionalism in the Police Service focuses upon the development of police officers who are free to make informed professional judgements that are guided by professional standards and social norms. This process requires the integration of lifelong learning into police practices in order to foster a more inclusive and reflective community of practice.

Have a look at the following case study and think about the following questions again:

- *What are the ethical considerations you need to think about here?*

- *What does the law require?*

- *What do personal ethics require?*

- *What do the public want you to do?*

- *You witness a fellow officer using excessive force to subdue a suspect. The suspect is well known to the police and has used violence against other officers in the past which leads you to condone the action. On returning to the police station later you find out that the suspect has suffered serious injuries which the officer involved denies any responsibility for. What do you do?*

This case study raises a multitude of competing ethical issues. The wide discretionary powers that police officers have make good judgement and decision making essential; yet the lack of clarity that surrounds this decision making process draws police officers towards, and often across, the boundaries of respectability (Waddington, 1999). The issue of ethics and decision making is problematic when attempting to define the acceptable use of force. For example, Neyroud highlights the moral dilemmas involved in using force where the individual officer has both a duty *to accord dignity and personal autonomy to every individual* (2008, page 684) while also having a duty to protect other individuals from the potential threat posed by that individual. The use of force must *be ethically justified as being proportionate to the threat and absolutely necessary in the terms of article 2 of the European Convention on Human Rights* (ibid., page 685). These moral and legal interpretations of the case study above attempt to provide some clarity, but most police officers decisions are made in a context where they are also informed by other factors such as risk avoidance and group loyalty. Therefore, we must return to a focus on police culture. Research evidence from across the globe has shown that, over a period of time, the focus on ethical policing values which is evident in the thinking of new police officers is gradually replaced by a more short-term and practical focus which is informed by local cultural values.

Ethics and police culture

The criminological literature on police culture has pointed towards the role of cynicism and pragmatism in providing clarity for police officers when they enter these ethically muddy waters. Cynicism encourages a practical rather than ethical approach to policing and erodes aspects of policing that come to be seen as ideological over time. This includes areas such as:

- Professionalism.

- Commitment to public service.

- Values such as policing by consent.

- Community engagement.

(Kleinig, 1996)

These values are replaced by a more pragmatic emphasis on local culture, or *the way things are done round here* (Robbins, 1990). The literature also indicates that these values can be replaced by a more pragmatic set of values that justify decisions that have already been made rather than a set of standards that guide an officer's actions (Fielding, 1988). These are the dangers that are presented by a focus on utilitarianism or 'the ends justify the means' and the potential route it presents into 'noble cause' corruption.

Hunt and Manning (1991) have demonstrated how police lying and the nature of police work, and officers' responses to it, open up a moral and practical minefield. For street-level cops, it generates an environment where illegitimate behaviour and the abuse of the rule of law can become accepted. In some cases 'lying' can be perceived as good police work (e.g. when this decreases the stress on victims' families or when conducting undercover work). Indeed, lying can be viewed as something that has to be learnt in order to become a successful police officer. This is the ethical trap that faces police officers who make poor decisions and find themselves defending actions that they know are wrong. Furthermore, these decisions can lead police officers towards misconduct and, where this behaviour persists, corruption.

Organisational accountability and police legitimacy

The collective impact of the actions of individual officers is central to understanding police legitimacy. The highly visible role that police officers play as gatekeepers to the criminal justice system, coupled with their powers to use force and restrict a person's liberty, means that clear and transparent organisational accountability structures are required to maintain public support for the work they do. Public support is an essential component of efficient policing and levels of public confidence in the police are directly linked to the attitudes and behaviour demonstrated by the police towards the public (Neyroud and Beckley, 2001). As policing in the UK is founded upon the democratic principles of policing by consent, public support for the police is an essential component of police legitimacy.

The latter part of the twentieth century presented considerable challenges to the authority and legitimacy of the Police Service in the UK (Scarman, 1982; MacPherson, 1999; Patten, 1999). The Scarman Report (1982) into the disturbances in Brixton in 1981 recommended radical reforms and proved to be a pivotal point in police–community relations. The reforms included the introduction of police–community consultation groups and a new complaints board, the Police Complaints Authority (PCA), which aimed to re-build public trust in the police's organisational accountability structures. The MacPherson Report (1999) criticised the lack of progress made by the Scarman reforms and the enduring problem of police relations with minority ethnic communities as well as the lack of an independent system of complaints (see also Patten, 1999).

In response to this, independent advisory groups were introduced to increase transparency in the police policy-making process while also seeking to involve a much broader range of lay advisers. The PCA was replaced by the Independent Police Complaints Commission (IPCC) in 2004. The initial aim of the IPCC was to construct a transparent and easily accessible system of redress for members of the public that re-built and maintained public support for the police and allowed the Police Service to explain its actions in controversial cases. The impact of the IPCC and the enhanced focus on standards is visible in official statistics compiled since the turn of the millennium. In 2004–05 the number of complaints recorded was 22,898 which represented a 44 per cent increase from the year before the establishment of the IPCC (IPCC, 2009). Since then, there has been a steady rise in the number of complaints received by the police up to a total of 53,534 in 2008–09 (ibid.). Internal misconduct issues remain a concern and in some quarters are viewed as the inevitable by-product of the police's status and powers (Waddington, 1999). The ongoing necessity of counteracting internal issues of malpractice and corruption remains a 'real one' (HMIC, 2006, page 13; Hughes, 2010).

Additional complications for organisational accountability and police legitimacy have been presented by the role of performance indicators since they were introduced in the 1994 Police and Magistrates Court Act. Initially, performance indicators and league tables sought to provide government and the public with a clear means of measuring the performance of their police force to ensure policing was efficient, effective and equitable but it has proved difficult to construct performance indicators that are meaningful to the public and which cover the broad range of tasks that the police are expected to fulfil. Indeed, evidence has shown that the focus on performance indicators has drawn police officers away from some of their core functions and towards more trivial tasks (Neyroud, 2008) thus proving to be counter-productive. This resulted in the Liberal–Conservative government removing all of the police's performance targets when they came to power in May 2010.

It is now time to think again about the two questions that were set at the beginning of this chapter.

- *Why is it important for police officers to be aware of ethical issues in their day-to-day work?*

- *How does poor police practice undermine police legitimacy?*

Have your responses to the questions changed after having read the chapter? If so, how have they changed?

CHAPTER SUMMARY

This chapter has pointed to a number of common changes that are taking place in policing across the globe. A broad consensus has developed in the (mainly Western) world that places some similar philosophical assumptions at the core of thinking about developments in policing. These include the following.

- The Police Service is going through a process of professionalisation.

- Policing requires community involvement.

- Pro-active and preventive strategies that focus on problem-solving are most successful (see Chapter 3).

The shift to professionalisation raises several important issues, namely police discretion, the role of training and education, standards of professional conduct and self-regulation. Historically, the Police Service in the UK (and in many other countries) has maintained discipline through a system of strict rules and punishments, as embodied in the old system of complaints and discipline. The new system of professional standards views police professionals as individuals who are highly trained and work alongside the community to build confidence in the Police Service while also developing technical skills that are able to assist crime reduction. These police officers demonstrate individual responsibility and high standards of conduct alongside a clear engagement with the ethics of operational policing.

Therefore, one common theme is that police forces across the globe are in the process of becoming a 'Police Service'. Thus far, this process is incomplete as police institutions make the shift from a militarised, hierarchical and coercive model of policing to a customer-orientated service model. This process requires significant changes in the way that police officers are trained. This is because traditional police training focuses upon competencies (or, 'doing things right') rather than ethical decision making ('doing the right things for the right reasons'). The ethical demands placed on the police are not intrinsically different from those placed on the rest of us but they are shaped by the police's right to use force as well as the organisational contexts that individual police officers work in. While police training has traditionally focused on legal perspectives on police work a greater emphasis is now being placed upon an appreciation of the social impact of police work and the important role of police ethics in decision making.

Ethical policing is most easily demonstrated through professional practice that is efficient, transparent and carried out with operational integrity. It is participative policing which is responsive to communities and able to incorporate this consultative approach into a cycle of reflective practice. The commodification of policing in Western societies has led to ever-increasing demand for policing services and the privatisation of policing functions in many countries. This has added impetus to police reform due to the recognition that competition presents a potential threat to both the legitimacy and authority of the public police. Attempts to improve police legitimacy through organisational accountability are also made more complex by the growth in plural policing at the local level (see Chapter 6) and trans-national policing at the global level (see Chapter 8), thus making it even more difficult for the public police to differentiate themselves from other service providers. By adopting an ethical code similar to that which exists in other professions the Police Service is able to differentiate itself from its market-driven competitors in the private security industry by emphasising its focus on the public good ahead of private profit.

High-profile police failures such as those documented in the Scarman and MacPherson Reports or the more recent death of Ian Tomlinson at the G20 protests highlight the importance of individual decision making for police legitimacy. Over two decades of research have provided the Police Service in the UK with an evidence-base that has questioned the effectiveness of traditional policing strategies in reducing crime. Rising fear of crime and an enhanced concern with victimisation coupled with the globalised threats of terrorism and trans-national organised crime have led to similar complex demands being made on nation-states by their citizens. The next chapter will look at the changing nature of crime, criminal justice and policing in the twentieth century and introduce you to the theories of globalisation that helps us make sense of these changes.

FURTHER READING

The application of ethics to police practice is discussed in much more detail in Neyroud and Beckley's (2001) *Policing, Ethics and Human Rights* as well as John Kleinig's (1996) *The Ethics of Policing.* Neyroud also provides an overview of the literature on police ethics in his chapter in Tim Newburn's (2008) *Handbook of Policing*, 2nd edition. The practical implications of ethical issues in policing are discussed in more detail in Brian Stout's (2010) *Equality and Diversity in Policing.*

REFERENCES

Alderson, J (1998) *Principled Policing: Protecting the Public with Integrity.* Winchester: Waterside Press.

Council of Europe (2001) *European Code of Police Ethics.* Strasbourg: Council of Europe Publishing.

Council of Europe (2010) *Manual on Human Rights Education with Young People.* Available online at www.eycb.coe.int/compass/en/pdf/6_7.pdf (Accessed 17 September 2010).

Fielding, N (1988) *Joining Forces: Police training, Socialisation and Occupational Competence.* London: Routledge.

Flanagan, R (2008) *The Review of Policing.* London: HMIC.

Her Majesty's Inspectorate of Constabulary (1999) *Police Integrity: Securing and Maintaining Public Confidence.* London: HMIC.

Her Majesty's Inspectorate of Constabulary (2006) *Raising the Standard: A Thematic Inspection of Professional Standards.* London: HMIC.

Home Office (1993) *Police Reform: A Police Service for the Twenty-First Century.* Cm2281. White Paper. London: HMSO.

Home Office (1998) *Crime and Disorder Act.* London: OPSI.

Home Office (2009) *Protecting the Public: Supporting the Public to Succeed.* Cm7749. White Paper. London: HMSO.

Hughes, M (2010) Root Out Corrupt Officers, Police Told. *The Independent.* Available online at www.independent.co.uk/news/uk/crime/root-out-corrupt-officers-police-told-1898139.html (Accessed 12 August 2010).

Hunt, J and Manning, P (1991) The Social Context of Police Lying. *Symbolic Interaction.* 14(1): 1–20.

Independent Police Complaints Commission (2009) *Police Complaints: Statistics for England and Wales.* Available online at www.ipcc.gov.uk/complaints_statistics_2008_09–3.pdf (Accessed 13 August 2010).

Independent Police Complaints Commission (2010) *Standards of Professional Behaviour.* Available online at www.ipcc.gov.uk/index/complaints/police_professional_standards/stand-ofprofbehaviour.htm (Accessed 29 July 2010).

Johnston, L and Shearing, C (2003) *Governing Security: Explorations in Policing and Justice.* London: Routledge.

Kleinig, J (1996) *The Ethics of Policing.* Cambridge: Cambridge University Press.

Locke, J (1690/1966) *Second Treatise of Government.* Oxford: Blackwell.

MacPherson, Lord (1999) *The Stephen Lawrence Inquiry.* London: Home Office.

Metropolitan Police (2010a) *Metropolitan Police: Mission and Values.* Available online at www.met.police.uk/about/mission.htm (Accessed 29 July 2010).

Metropolitan Police (2010b) *History of the Metropolitan Police.* Available online at www.met.police.uk/history/definition.htm (Accessed 2 August 2010).

Neyroud, P (2008) Policing and ethics, In Newburn, T (ed) *Handbook of Policing.* Cullompton: Willan.

Neyroud, P and Beckley, A (2001) *Policing, Ethics and Human Rights*. Cullompton: Willan.

Patten, C (1999) *A New Beginning: Policing in Northern Ireland*. Available online at www.cain.ulst.ac.uk/issues/police/patten/patten99.pdf (Accessed 2 August 2010).

Robbins, S P (1990) *Organisation Theory: Structure, Design and Applications*. New Jersey: Prentice Hall International.

Scarman, Lord (1982) *The Brixton Disorders: 10th–12th April 1981*. London: HMSO.

Starmer, K (1999) *European Human Rights Law: The Human Rights Act 1998 and the European Convention on Human Rights*. London: Legal Action Group.

Stout, B (2010) *Equality and Diversity in Policing*. Exeter: Learning Matters.

Thames Valley Police (2010) *About Us*. Available online at www.thamesvalley.police.uk/aboutus/aboutus-stplan.htm. (Accessed 2 August 2010).

Waddington, P A J (1999) *Policing Citizens*. London: UCL Press.

USEFUL WEBSITES

http://cain.ulst.ac.uk/issues/police/patten/patten99.pdf

www.coe.int/t/e/legal_affairs/legal_co-operation/police_and_internal_security/documents/Rec(2001)10_ENG4831–7.pdf

www.eycb.coe.int/compass/en/pdf/6_7.pdf

www.ipcc.gov.uk/Pages/default.aspx

www.met.police.uk/history/definition.htm

www.thamesvalley.police.uk/aboutus/aboutus-stplan.htm

8   The globalisation of policing

CHAPTER OBJECTIVES

By the end of this chapter you should be able to:

- understand the changing global context that influences patterns of crime and policing responses;
- understand a range of different theories related to the globalisation of crime and policing;
- identify the main transitions enacted by the globalisation of policing;
- understand the implications of globalisation for police practice.

LINKS TO STANDARDS

This chapter provides opportunities for links with the following Skills for Justice National Occupational Standards (NOS) for Policing and Law Enforcement 2008:

AA1   Promote equality and foster diversity.
AB1   Communicate effectively with people.
AE1   Maintain and develop your own knowledge, skills and competence.
CA1   Use law enforcement actions in a fair and justified way.

Introduction

Both the Police Service (as an institution) and policing (as a process of maintaining social order) are often viewed in a local and parochial way – as something that is particular to each individual nation-state and as a specific aspect of state sovereignty. While to some extent this local focus is important, the processes of globalisation coupled with the increasingly global scope of criminality and threats to security have limited the criminological value of this perspective. Harvey (1989) defines globalisation as the compression of time and space through new modes of communication, trade and travel. Criminology's inability to make sense of the impact of globalisation has meant that attempts to appreciate the global context of crime and policing have often been labelled as comparative or sometimes even 'foreign' (Bayley, 1999). Yet, the broad processes of globalisation have also impacted upon the nature of crime and the demands of policing at the local level, thus making a focus on trans-national crimes and international police cooperation increasingly important. These social changes have produced new demands for police officers, increasing the complexity of the police role and requiring a more advanced skill-base. A greater focus on international cooperation is now required and key global issues such as human rights and trans-national crimes have relevance at the local level for police officers. This should not come as a surprise. Policing in democratic societies takes place within a socio-political landscape that acknowledges the importance of social justice, social cohesion, fairness, equity and human rights and this means that social change affects police institutions across the globe in similar ways.

PRACTICAL TASK

Before you read on any further have a think about the following question and note down your first thoughts.

* *Why is it important for policing students and police officers to be aware of global issues?*

The changing global context of crime

Prior to the terrorist attacks in the US on 11 September 2001, the greatest threat to security in Europe was considered to be uncontrolled immigration. The fall of the Berlin Wall in 1989 had been interpreted by some commentators as symbolising the end of ideological and political conflict across the developed world and this led to a new focus on trans-national organised crime which had proliferated under the free market conditions of globalisation. Within the policing context, the term 'trans-national' refers to police cooperation that takes place across national boundaries. At the global level new links were becoming apparent between organised crime and international terrorism and this enhanced the global focus on trans-national organised crime. Trans-national organised crime is an American term that dates back to the organised crime of the prohibition era of the 1920s and 1930s and has subsequently been exported to other countries. The initial focus on the illegal trafficking of alcohol widened to include gambling, drugs and prostitution. Illicit drugs and human trafficking (trans-national prostitution) remain significant international problems today and attempts to respond to these illegal markets have driven developments in global policing.

In contrast to those who foresaw an end to ideological conflict after 1989, the UK has witnessed the rise of radical Islamism (as a comparatively invisible force throughout the 1990s and more visibly since 11 September 2001 and the subsequent wars in Afghanistan and Iraq) and the acceleration of trans-national policing responses to this threat. Under these circumstances, issues of crime and security have become conflated and shifted the responsibility for trans-national crime, immigration and terrorism to security agencies. Post–cold war definitions of security now include legal, political, social and economic issues. The concept of freedom has been re-moulded and is increasingly equated with security and as 'freedom from threat'. National and international policing and border agencies regulate the movement of migrants and asylum seekers and cite the 'war on terror' and the 'war on drugs' to garner support for exclusionary policies. Three important factors have driven this process:

> *The changing economic market (particularly in the European Union (EU) but also through the North American Free Trade Agreement (NAFTA), the World Trade Organisation (WTO), and the International Monetary Fund (IMF).*

The opening up of the global market in goods has made it easier for people to be distributed and re-distributed across the world. Cheap travel, easy access to global communications (previously restricted to the military) and 24-hour multi-media output have made the world seem smaller. This has facilitated simultaneous growth in cross-border crimes.

The globalisation of specific crimes

The internationalisation of certain crimes that are no longer confined to particular nation-states such as terrorism, trafficking (drugs; people; animal; arts/antiquities; arms), fraud, money laundering, cybercrimes and industrial espionage.

The need for more cross-border police cooperation

Common social changes across Western countries have decreased the public's tolerance of everyday crime and signs of disorder as well as the perceived inadequacies of policing and other criminal justice responses. This has led to an extended focus on signal crimes and anti-social behaviour (Innes, 2010), policing strategies that engage communities and the language of zero tolerance. Both the ideological underpinning and the rhetoric of community policing and zero tolerance come from an Anglo-American model that has been exported across the globe, often as part of packages of financial aid.

Sociologists and criminologists have tried to make sense of this changing global context and the impact that it has had on crime, disorder and perceptions thereof. It is commonly acknowledged that economic and cultural changes driven by globalisation, new technologies and mass consumerism have reconfigured the contours and structures of the Western world (Bauman, 2000; Giddens, 1990). A heightened awareness among the global public of threats to security and order, in part infused through a 24/7 mass media, has increased demand for security and led to a pluralisation of policing providers from the commercial, statutory and voluntary sectors. The expansion of the private security industry since the 1950s coupled with the acceleration of public sector reforms in many Western, neoliberal countries since the 1980s have been seen by some as representing a re-structuring of policing (Bayley and Shearing, 2001) and an acknowledgement of the limits of sovereign states in providing sufficient security for an increasingly anxious public (Garland, 1996).

The processes of globalisation, in particular global capitalism, have encouraged the police to shed some of their traditional functions (see Chapter 6) as political elites opened up a competitive market for public services that impacted upon local policing from the 1990s onwards (Home Office, 1993; 1994; 1995). The pluralisation of policing provision also led to the public police re-asserting their symbolic and sovereign authority in other areas. In response to the growing powers of trans-national policing agencies, the UK government established the Serious and Organised Crime Agency (SOCA) in 2005 to lead the response to global and trans-national crime problems and to re-assert the role of the UK nation-state police at the European and global levels (Cope et al., 1997). SOCA centralised control over cross-border policing within a structure where it was accountable only to the Home Secretary rather than to the three parties of the tri-partite structure of police accountability. SOCA is due to be replaced by the National Crime Agency in 2013 at which point it will take on additional responsibilities from the UK Border Agency and potentially extend its crime-fighting function into border management and areas more traditionally associated with customs and excise. The complex structures of police governance with their local, national, European and international strands are demonstrative of a more diverse policing structure than witnessed for most of the twentieth century and are reflective of post-modern changes across Western societies more generally.

Within this climate of uncertainty and complex policing structures, nation-states have tried to re-assert their symbolic sovereign power through the use of 'tough' symbolic language coupled with an intensification of law and order policies. Zero-tolerance policing in the US during the 1990s, the UK's focus on anti-social behaviour from 1997 onwards, the tough language of excluding disorderly youth in France that helped make Sarkozy president in 2007, and the exclusionary rhetoric faced by Muslim youth in the Netherlands over the past decade have all provided examples of the rise of an exclusionary logic and criminological 'othering' in wealthy Western countries. All these are examples of weakened nation-states attempting to re-assert a sense of order and wield their sovereign power over those seen as presenting a threat to the voting public.

PRACTICAL TASK

Have a look in the SOCA's library (www.soca.gov.uk/about-soca/library) to evaluate the threat of global crime against the UK. Which areas do the SOCA reports identify as presenting the greatest threat to communities in the UK?

Policing in a global context

As a consequence of the changes outlined in the previous section it has become commonplace, although not uncontested, within the criminological study of policing to put forward the idea that public police forces have lost their monopoly of control over policing post-modern societies (Johnston, 1999; Bayley and Shearing, 2001; Jones and Newburn, 2002; Stenson, 2005). For example, in the UK we have policing provided by commercial organisations, local councils (city ambassadors, traffic wardens), individuals and the state. A plural kaleidoscope of agencies also carry out policing functions at the international level. These include private military and security companies and policing agencies such as Interpol and Europol. This means that traditional structures in policing are being challenged from both above and below in states that require enhanced levels of security but are either unable or unwilling to provide it. The dominance of neoliberal ideologies (weak states–strong markets) has driven many of these changes in Western democracies. This presents a potential future where market strength could determine levels of security in societies, particularly in urban areas (Davis, 1990; 2002), a process that is likely to undermine the future provision of equitable forms of justice.

Because of this, understanding twenty-first century policing requires analysis of the dialectic (or relationship) between the global and the local (Giddens, 1990, page 64). Tension between policing, security and order maintenance at the local, national and international levels has made it difficult to police a more diverse and ambiguous society with competing demands and needs. In some areas this has produced a police identity crisis and raised the question about the effectiveness of the police in controlling crime. This is evident in current debates about police objectives, strategies, organisation, management, discipline and accountability. In response to this, a 2005 report by Her Majesty's Inspectorate of Constabulary titled 'Closing the Gap' argued that public policing in England and Wales should be restructured to meet present-day demands for policing security at the local, national and international levels. In the words of the then commissioner of the London Metropolitan Police, Sir Ian Blair: *National security depends on neighbourhood security… It is not the police and intelligence agencies who will defeat crime and terror …; it is communities* (BBC News, 2005).

As we noted earlier, the catalyst for recent growth in trans-national policing has been the 11 September 2001 terrorist attacks in the US and the subsequent high-profile attacks in European cities such as Madrid, London and Istanbul. The indirect consequence of these developments is that security issues have come to dominate the policing agenda ahead of those of governance and accountability, and this is most obvious when looking at the development of largely unaccountable supra-national agencies such as Europol. A separation is taking place between those who authorise policing and those who carry out the policing role. Both these functions are gradually shifting away from government – a process referred to as 'multi-lateralisation' (Bayley and Shearing, 2001). The power of supra-national policing agencies such as Europol is increasing and presenting a potential threat to the actions and independence of state agencies and the sovereignty of individual states.

Policing, surveillance and security: theoretical explanations

An enhanced awareness of uncertainty and risk in Western societies has led to growth in the problems faced by policing agencies (Beck, 1992) where crime and deviance are viewed as technical problems that require management through *procedures and technologies – classification schemes, probability calculations etc* (Ericson and Haggerty, 1997, page 39). Thus, the focus on risk in the 'information age' (see Castells, 1996–98) has made policing increasingly dependent upon the production of intelligence and the role of police officers as 'knowledge workers' (Ericson and Haggerty, 1997). Attempts to manage problems of security are increasingly directed through new surveillance technologies as much as traditional forms of policing. Most obviously, this can be seen in attempts to manage the mobility of groups and individuals through new modes of surveillance such as closed circuit television, passenger name records and biometrics. This surveillance functions through a network of public and private trans-national databases and agencies that extends beyond the jurisdiction of traditional policing agencies and includes border agencies, airline carriers and commercial databases.

The technologisation of UK policing and security began during 'the Troubles' in Northern Ireland with the Irish Republican Army during the late 1960s, before drifting into crime prevention throughout the 1980s and 1990s and back to (international) terrorism as the twenty-first century began. Because attempts to manage security threats encompass a wide range of areas (crime, terrorism, immigration, asylum, welfare), identification technologies have become a central feature of security policies (e.g. identity databases or iris scans at airports) and have crept into everyday life. This is what Bigo (1994) calls the 'security continuum' – a means of using policing and surveillance technologies to target not only offenders but migrants, asylum seekers and anyone else who fits into the 'other' category. This surveillance creep ultimately targets the entire population, sorting different social groups according to the risk they are deemed to present to society (Lyon, 2002).

The integration of security devices into policing and wider society is fostered by the interconnection of three logics (Bigo, 1994):

- A logic of security that corresponds to the identification of risks and dangers, most obviously risky and dangerous people.

- A logic of management flows that corresponds to the mobility of people, trade, and transport.

- A logic of ambient intelligence that integrates microprocessors into the daily life of individuals through social networking, mobile phones and internet use.

New technologies enable new modes and methods of police cooperation across the globe through mutually accessible databases, bi-lateral and multi-lateral agreements, and new supra-national modes of governance that operate above nation-states through organisations such as the European Union, the United Nations, and the North Atlantic Treaty Organisation (NATO). The next section introduces you to the most prominent forms of international police cooperation and trans-national policing organisations.

CASE STUDY

Have a look at the following document from the National Police Improvement Agency (2009) about the use of the automatic number plate recognition system: www.acpo.police.uk/asp/policies/Data/ANPR_genesis.pdf.

- *What benefits does this technology offer the police in tracking offenders?*

- *What are the potential problems that may occur when using this technology against ordinary members of the public (see section three in the document)?*

Have a look at the following document from the European Union (2007) about the use of the Passenger Name Record: http://europa.eu/rapid/pressReleasesAction. do?reference=MEMO/07/294&format=HTML&aged=0&language=EN.

- *What role does this technology play in assisting police cooperation?*

- *What are the potential problems that may occur when using this technology against ordinary members of the public?*

Police cooperation across the globe

Police cooperation and trans-national policing are not new. The 1648 Treaty of Westphalia recognised the right of individual states to govern their own sovereign territory free from external threat and this recognition was accompanied by an acknowledgement of the mutual threats faced by European states. Most obviously, this included piracy (a continued threat in the twenty-first century), slavery (which has evolved into the contemporary crime of human trafficking) and a recognition of the existence of ungovernable zones in the high seas (which presaged the contemporary problem of governing cyberspace). A relatively high degree of internationalism and cross-border activity, often aided by global communication systems and technologies, can be found in many present-day organised crime groups and are therefore required in police responses. Despite this, international police developments are often driven by bureaucratisation trends in national police agencies (Deflem, 2003) and the availability of new technologies. Thus, the cooperative structure of international and trans-national policing agencies shines a light on the characteristics and limitations of individual agencies. As the previous section noted, technological developments, in particular the construction of databases, and concerns with efficiency have been the primary considerations in the development of international responses to organised crime and terrorism.

The growth in number of policing agencies, structures and forms of cooperation across the globe has made issues of governance and accountability more important. While functioning at the international or global levels, these agencies and structures are essentially trans-national as they help facilitate policing that takes place across borders. This raises a potential challenge to state sovereignty. Policing and internal security are central functions of the state as they relate to the right to use coercive force and maintain legitimate authority over a territory and population. Therefore, relinquishing control of this function is not something that states do without due consideration. Furthermore, the proliferation of global policing agencies raises concerns for states and the public about how supra-national agencies and structures are governed and made accountable for their actions.

It is the development of supra-national, trans-national and international policing agencies, as highlighted in this chapter, that has encouraged criminologists to talk about a post-modern police that extends beyond the state as well as a new era for policing at the global level that complements the reforms and re-structuring at the local level that we have outlined in previous chapters. Trans-national plural policing agencies raise further issues of governance and accountability that are yet to be resolved. In particular, the expansion of private policing amidst a lack of public accountability and transparency has been raised in twenty-first century war zones such as Iraq and Afghanistan. The growth of international private military companies to supplement, and in many cases replace, the armed forces of a multitude of nation-states has brought the role of private policing agencies into question, particularly in areas of political conflict such as Guantanamo Bay and the West Bank.

From the formation of the International Police Commission, now known as Interpol, in 1923, policing in North America and Europe has always had a trans-national element to it, but in recent years this international focus has intensified. Understanding trans-national policing and other global influences within twenty-first century criminology is important as the enforcement of the law and the right to use coercive force within specific borders is one of the defining features of sovereign nations. Since the 11 September 2001 attacks in the US and the ascension of the Schengen accord in Europe, border controls have become viewed as a key weakness in global security. A by-product of the development of borderless economies has been an increase in trans-national crime and policing. So, while the WTO and agreements such as the General Agreement on Tariffs and Subsidies (GATS) and NAFTA have created a global free market in goods and services, the threats to security that have developed simultaneously have resulted in the expansion of organisations such as Interpol and Europol, both through greater cooperation and greater powers. The following sections outline the important role played by international policing agencies in combating global crime.

Interpol

Interpol is the most obvious example of trans-national policing as the organisation seeks to promote police cooperation across national boundaries. Interpol's role involves promoting mutual assistance between policing agencies within the limits of national laws and the Universal Declaration of Human Rights. The organisation was originally established in Vienna in 1923 as the International Police Commission but the outbreak of the Second World War resulted in its closure. Interpol re-emerged as a new entity after the Second World War with a headquarters in Paris and its modernised constitution was formally recognised in 1956. Interpol's central headquarters are now in Lyon, France, and the agency works with 186 policing agencies and employs around 200 staff. Interpol's main concerns are with public safety, terrorism, organised crime, illicit drugs, weapons smuggling, human trafficking, money laundering, financial and other high-tech crimes and corruption.

Interpol had been slowly expanding its anti-terrorist activities since the 1970s but the impact of the 11 September 2001 attacks in the US provided added momentum for its growth. Interpol has developed a reputation for providing warnings about potential terrorist attacks although it deals with all types of criminal activity. Member agencies are meant to contact Interpol in the wake of a terrorist attack and provide details concerning what took place. Interpol subsequently issues international notices for fugitive terrorists whose arrest is sought. Interpol also deals with the financing of terrorism as the frequency and seriousness of terrorist attacks is directly related to the amount of funding that groups receive.

Interpol issues

- Red Notices – for the arrest and extradition of a suspect.
- Blue Notices – for information about a suspect.
- Green Notices – contain information about a suspect for circulation.
- Yellow Notices – contain details about missing persons.
- Black Notices – relate to unidentified bodies.
- Orange Notices – provide warnings about dangerous materials.

There have been persistent doubts about the security of Interpol's communications network. Interpol is only as effective as the trust put in it by its members, and many of these nations regard it as slow and ineffective. This was evident in the US' response to the 11 September 2001 attacks when Interpol was excluded from the initial investigation. More trivial examples are also available: red notices which you would assume to be urgent used to be issued by the cheapest form of postal mail. Interpol's main role is to promote collaboration through efficient procedures of information exchange and intelligence gathering with all 186 countries although it is perceived to be strongly influenced by the US and Europe. Interpol is not a supra-national policing agency as it has no investigative powers.

Europol

Because Interpol was not initially perceived to be successful in tackling terrorism, 12 European states came together to establish the TREVI Group in 1975 which developed a rapid and secure communications system for collecting and disseminating information about terrorism and terrorists. This structure was formalised in the arrangements made for the EU under the 1992 Maastricht Treaty. The Maastricht Treaty came into force on 1 November 1993 and placed policing issues under its third pillar, 'Justice and Home Affairs', which identified the EU as an area of 'freedom, security and justice'. This meant that the TREVI Group was ultimately subsumed into the European Drugs Unit, Europol's predecessor, which was established in 1993. The main aim of Europol, which became fully operational on 1 July 1999, is to promote cooperation between law enforcement agencies in the EU. Europol also handles intelligence, carries out crime analysis and promotes the harmonisation of investigative techniques across Europe through the Europol Computer System (TECS).

Europol's mandate incorporates all serious forms of international crime, including international terrorism since the 1999 Amsterdam Treaty. Europol's main responsibilities are in the areas of trafficking (drugs, vehicles, human beings, guns), child pornography, money laundering and terrorism. In 2002, Europol's mandate was extended to permit liaison with other international bodies (such as Interpol and non-EU states such as Norway, Iceland, Canada and the US) through bi-lateral agreements. But Europol provides no specific information about its collaborative and investigative work. This means that it is not accountable to any of the individual states that it operates within, unlike national or regional policing agencies. Europol is supported by Eurojust which performs similar co-ordination functions to Europol for prosecution agencies as well as Frontex (the EU border police) and CEPOL (the EU police college).

Europol is distinctive from other global policing agencies as it was not formed (from the bottom-up) by police professionals, but was the result of a (top-down) decision by the political and legislative body of the EU. Despite this, Europol is not an executive police force and does not have autonomous investigative powers. Europol is an international, rather than trans-national, policing agency, as it represents the EU and is not held directly to account by any elected public. This means that is differs in form from Interpol as it is a relatively autonomous body that acts beyond the state and thus has its own supra-national political remit. This represents a challenge to the independent sovereignty of each of the EU states and raises questions about the governance and accountability of supra-national policing agencies. This challenge to state sovereignty has been evident in resistance to the role of Europol from some nation-states.

PRACTICAL TASK

Visit Europol's website (www.europol.eu.int/) to evaluate their aims and objectives.

REFLECTIVE TASK

Visit Statewatch's website (www.statewatch.org) and search around their database for a different perspective on the aims and objectives of Europol. Why are Statewatch suspicious about the aims and objectives of Europol?

The Schengen Agreement

In addition to the development of horizontal interaction between trans-national and international policing agencies, the latter part of the twentieth century also bore witness to growth in vertical police–state interaction, as exemplified in the Schengen Agreement (den Boer, 1999). On 14 June 1985, Belgium, Germany, France, Luxembourg and the Netherlands agreed to eliminate border controls between their countries. This took place on the same day that the European Commission laid out its plans for a single European market. Denmark, Greece and the UK initially refused to sign the agreement. The agreement was implemented on 19 June 1990 with the creation of the Schengen Information System, a database that would share information on people, stolen vehicles, identity cards and other data from all member states. By 1998, 13 of the existing 15 EU member states had signed up to the Schengen Agreement which abolished border controls but maintained security through agreements about external border controls and improved police and judicial cooperation.

The Treaty of Amsterdam incorporated the Schengen arrangements into the body of EU law on 1 May 1999 while simultaneously extending the powers of Europol. The UK and Ireland remain outside Schengen although, on 29 May 2000 and 1 April 2002 respectively, both countries were granted permission to participate in police and legal cooperation in criminal matters such as the pursuit of offenders over borders as well as the trafficking of drugs. The Schengen Agreement permits covert police action and cross-border collaboration as well as providing the basis for the Schengen Information System (SIS) database. SIS has subsequently become part of a much broader plan for a European Information System (EIS) which is linked to the development of Europol.

Having read this chapter and the previous chapter on plural policing, do you think it can be argued that the public police have lost their monopoly over policing provision in the UK? Further, if this is the case, to what extent are we seeing the emergence of new global policing providers?

Criminology and the globalisation of policing

This chapter has identified a number of emergent themes. First, the processes of globalisation have reformulated the contours of crime, in particular organised crime, at the local, national and global level. This has led to similar changes in the structure of policing. Criminologists have attempted to explain these developments through a language that incorporates an emphasis on risk and uncertainty as well as a recognition of policing as knowledge work in an information age. Within this changing context, an enhanced emphasis has been placed on police cooperation and new policing agencies have emerged that operate at the transnational, international and supra-national levels. This raises questions about the structure of police governance and accountability at the local, national and international levels and whether this can provide legitimacy and trust for citizens across the globe. In addition to this, studying the globalisation of policing provides new insights into criminal behaviour as well as a comparative perspective on policing and other responses to crimes. Bayley (1999) outlines four key benefits that the global study of policing brings to students, academics, policy makers and practitioners across the globe. We have adapted these four areas into three sections of practical and reflective tasks for you to investigate issues raised in this chapter and to help make some clearer links between criminological theories and the globalisation of policing.

Extending knowledge of possibilities

We all have a tendency to believe that the way things are in our own country is normal. Police uniforms are normal. Policing strategies are normal. Police culture is normal. This can only be challenged through international comparative study; yet many nation-states seem unwilling to do this. The structures of policing in each state are rooted in deep social, cultural and historical traditions (such as policing by consent, the importance of officer discretion and constabulary independence) and cannot be changed without careful consideration. But still, policing can be reformed and developed using comparative study. New technological systems (e.g. Compstat; Airwave) can be brought in from abroad as can training and investigative techniques, management systems and forensic analysis.

The National Institute of Justice in the US does not fund foreign study while the Home Office in England and Wales funds a range of comparative if not expressly foreign work. In Japan, police officers are sent abroad on a regular basis as part of their development. In Europe generally, countries have been forced into a more collaborative approach because of their close proximity and the ease with which European citizens can cross borders. This was first acknowledged in the 1975 TREVI Agreement, which recognised the mutual operational requirements of many European police forces, and subsequently in the Schengen Agreement and the developing role of Europol. While there are few databanks of global policing knowledge, the United Nations Criminal Justice Information Network, which is based at the University of Vienna, collects data and provides links to data sources from a multitude of countries (see below).

PRACTICAL TASK

Visit the United Nations Criminal Justice Information Network's website (www. uncjin.org/) and identify the different data sources that are available to help you undertake comparative studies of policing in different countries.

Developing insights into the relationship between policing and society

It is important to remember that crime is socially constructed within each nation-state and policing is governmentally constructed within each nation-state. Understanding this requires international comparative criminological study. Generating a historical and comparative understanding of international policing remains one of the key challenges facing criminologists at this time. The rise of global terrorism, global trafficking systems and cyberspace caught governments, police practitioners and academics by surprise. In the UK, recent debate has revolved around police reform and attempts to restore links with the community (see Chapter 5). In part, this has been a response to the development of less transparent policing agencies operating at the national and international level, such as the Serious Organised Crime Agency (SOCA) and Europol. These policing agencies are tasked with policing drug trafficking, people trafficking, money laundering and terrorism and work at a distance from the public and alongside global policing agencies and the security services. New modes of policing and surveillance often involve secretive (or poorly explained and misunderstood), covert practices that can seem similar to those of police agencies in dictatorships. In liberal democracies, the growing anxieties about the effects of globalisation, inequality, population movements and demographic complexity, terrorism, and the risks and insecurity that they bring have brought about burgeoning new powers to deal with these issues. In the effort to make policing more effective and hence improve our security against threats, a question is raised about the extent to which we are sacrificing the liberal rights and freedoms that distinguish the liberal democracies from dictatorships?

Criminological study can assist us in answering two key questions about the changing structure of policing in the twenty-first century.

- What impact do the police have on society? (A question for the police)

- What impact does society have on the police? (A question for criminologists)

This leads onto further questions, such as the following.

- Why do specific policing strategies work/not work in specific contexts?

- Can policing strategies be successfully transferred from one country to another?

- Can theories in policing/criminology be applied across the globe?

REFLECTIVE TASK

Consider the questions outlined above. What are the potential obstacles that the police face when transferring successful policing strategies such as community policing (neighbourhood and reassurance policing) from one country to another?

Gaining perspective on ourselves/increasing the chances for successful reform

A key area of concern for all democratic countries involves the quality of the relationship that the police have with civic society. Marenin (2005, page 101) argues that the provision of effective and equitable policing services (or the perception thereof) is a precondition of a democratic political structure. Ivkovic (2008) has demonstrated that public confidence in the police across jurisdictions is related to the quality of governance in each country as well as the contact individuals have with the police. A clear relationship has also been identified between the way policing is carried out and experienced by the public (procedural justice) and levels of public trust and confidence in the police (Hough et al., 2010). Public mistrust of the police in India provides a useful point of comparison here, with the low status and limited education of police officers being cited as two reasons for a lack of public confidence. This can be compared with countries such as England and Wales and the US where over three quarters of respondents to public confidence surveys stated that they thought the police were doing a good job (Ivkovic, 2008). Analysis of developments in policing at the local and global levels encourages us to re-evaluate the aims and objectives of policing within the context of contemporary social, economic and political changes.

REFLECTIVE TASK

Review the earlier chapters on the restoration of community policing and the development of plural policing to identify international influences on police reform in the UK.

C H A P T E R   S U M M A R Y

This chapter has provided an introduction to the influence that social, political, economic and cultural changes have had upon crime and policing across the globe. In particular, the threat of trans-national organised crime has been highlighted as well as the evolution of new and established policing agencies that operate at the local, national and international levels. This provides further context for understanding the reforms that have been taking place in policing in the UK over the past 30 years and the impact of global changes within local contexts. In the final chapter we turn our attention back to the UK and the likely shape of policing as we move further into the twenty-first century. This chapter considers the future patterns of policing and how the Police Service might be required to contribute to multi-agency initiatives alongside other policing and offender management agencies, as well as with active citizens.

FURTHER READING

Most policing textbooks have at least one chapter that introduces new readers to the subject of global or trans-national policing. More textbooks are now appearing that focus specifically on the global context that policing works within. Deflem's (2003) *Policing World Society* and den Boer's (1999) *Policing across the World* are two well-established examples of work in this area. Ericson and Haggerty's (1997) *Policing the Risk Society* remains a key theoretical referencing point and has relevance to developments in policing across the globe.

REFERENCES

Bauman, Z (2000) *Liquid Modernity*. Cambridge: Polity.

Bayley, D (1999) Policing: The World Stage, In Mawby, R (ed) *Policing Across the World: Issues for the Twenty-First Century*. London: UCL Press.

Bayley, D and Shearing, C (2001) *The New Structure of Policing: Description, Conceptualization and Research Agenda*. Washington: National Institute of Justice, Available online at www.ncjrs.org/pdffiles1/nij/187083.pdf (Accessed 20 December 2010).

Beck, U (1992) *Risk Society*. London: Sage.

Bigo, D (1994) The European Internal Security Field: Stakes and Rivalries in a Newly Developing Area of Police Intervention, in Anderson, M and den Boer, M (eds) *Policing Across National Boundaries*. London: Pinter.

Blair, I (2005) The Dimbleby Lecture. *BBC News*. Available online at http://news.bbc.co.uk/1/hi/uk/4443386.stm (Accessed 19 December 2010).

Castells, M (1996) *The Rise of the Network Society, The Information Age: Volume I*. Chichester: Wiley-Blackwell.

Cope, S, Leishman, F and Starie, P (1997) Globalization, new public management and the enabling state. *International Journal of Public Sector Management*, **10**(6): 444–60.

Davis, M (1990) *City of Quartz*. New York: Vintage.

Davis, M (2002) *Dead Cities*. New York: New Press.

Deflem, M (2003) *Policing World Society*. Oxford: Oxford University Press.

DenBoer, M (1999) Internationalization: A Challenge to Police Organizations in Europe, in Mawby, R (ed) *Policing across the World: Issues for the Twenty-First Century*. London: UCL Press.

Ericson, R and Haggerty, K (1997) *Policing the Risk Society*. Oxford: Clarendon Press.

Europa (2007) The Passenger Name Record: Frequently Asked Questions. *EU Press Releases*. Available online at http://europa.eu/rapid/pressReleasesAction.do?reference=MEMO/07/294&format=HTML&aged=0&language=EN (Accessed 19 December 2010).

Garland, D (1996) The Limits of the Sovereign State. *British Journal of Criminology*, **36**(4): 445–71.

Giddens, A (1990) *The Consequences of Modernity*. Cambridge: Polity.

Harvey, D (1989) *The Condition of Postmodernity*. Oxford: Blackwell.

Home Office (1993) *Inquiry into Police Responsibilities and Rewards (Sheehy Report)*. London: HMSO.

Home Office (1994) *Police and Magistrates Court Act*. London: HMSO.

Home Office (1995) *Review of Police Core and Ancillary Tasks (Posen Report)*. London: HMSO.

Hough, M, Jackson, J, Bradford, B, Myhill, A and Quinton, P (2010) Procedural justice, Trust and Institutional Legitimacy. *Policing: A Journal of Policy and Practice*, **4**(3): 203–10.

Innes, M (2010) Whatever Happened to Reassurance Policing? *Policing: A Journal of Policy of Practice*, 4(**3**): 225–32.

Ivkovic, S (2008) A Comparative Study of Public Support for the Police. *International Criminal Justice Review*, **18**(4): 406–34.

Johnston, L (2000) *Policing Britain*. Harlow: Longman.

Jones, T and Newburn, T (2002) The Transformation of Policing? Understanding Current Trends in Policing Systems. *British Journal of Criminology*, **42**(1): 129–46.

Lyon, D (2002) *Surveillance as Social Sorting: Privacy, Risk and Automated Discrimination*. London: Routledge.

Marenin, O (2005) Building a Global Police Studies Community. *Police Quarterly*, **8**(1): 99–136.

National Police Improvement Agency (2009) *Practical Advice on the Management and Use of Automatic Number Plate Recognition*. London: NPIA.

O'Connor, D (2005) *Closing the Gap: a Review of the 'Fitness for Purpose' of the Current Structure of Policing in England and Wales*. London: HMIC.

Stenson, K (2005) Sovereignty, Biopolitics and Community Safety in Britain. *Theoretical Criminology*, **9**(3): 265–87.

www.acpo.police.uk/asp/policies/Data/ANPR_genesis.pdf

www.europa.eu/rapid/pressReleasesAction.do?reference=MEMO/07/294&format=HTML&aged=0&language=EN

www.europol.eu.int/

www.interpol.int/

www.soca.gov.uk/about-soca/library

www.statewatch.org

www.uncjin.org/

Trans-National Policing Timeline

Over the past 30 years, there has been a rapid growth in trans-national policing structures and institutions in response to the globalisation of crime and security problems, yet these developments are by no means new.

1648	*The Treaty of Westphalia.*
1848	*The year of revolution' across Europe. For the first time, the potential for supra-national policing structures is discussed.*
1851	*Establishment of the Police Union of German States (dissolved in 1866).*
1923	*International Criminal Police Commission (later to become Interpol) established in Vienna. Aim: to act as a communication exchange.*
1938	*International Criminal Police Commission taken over by the Nazis prior to the start of the Second World War.*
1956	*International Criminal Police Commission re-launched as the International Criminal Police Office in France.*
1975	*Trevi Group established (tasked with counter terrorism, drug trafficking, organised crime and police training).*
1986	*Schengen Agreement established.*
1992	*Maastricht Treaty creates the 'common market', opening up European borders and creating new potential security threats.* *Police co-operation is integrated into the third pillar of Justice and Home Affairs, creating a supra-national level of policing governance.*
1993	*Creation of the Europol Drugs Unit (precursor to Europol).*
1995	*Legal convention for Europol signed. Aim: to share intelligence and conduct analysis of trans-national organised crime.*
1995	*Creation of the Schengen Information System (excludes UK and Ireland).*
1997	*Treaty of Amsterdam categorises EU countries as an 'Area of Freedom, Security and Justice'.*
1999	*Europol becomes fully operational – based in the Hague.*
2001	*Treaty of Nice establishes Eurojust.*
2009	*Treaty of Lisbon provides a further extension to the powers of Europol.*

9 Policing in the twenty-first century: towards the active community?

CHAPTER OBJECTIVES

By the end of this chapter you should be able to:

- identify how the role and function of the police changes in different social, political and cultural contexts;
- examine how criminological theories help us to predict the potential future shape of policing;
- understand the role of criminological study in researching the police and policing in the twenty-first century.

LINKS TO STANDARDS

This chapter provides opportunities for links with the following Skills for Justice, National Occupational Standards (NOS) for Policing and Law Enforcement 2008.

AB1   Communicate effectively with people.
AE1   Maintain and develop your own knowledge, skills and competence.
HA2   Manage your own resources and professional development.

Introduction

This final chapter discusses the likely shape of policing in the UK as we move further into the twenty-first century. In particular, the chapter considers how the Police Service might be required to contribute to multi-agency initiatives alongside other policing and offender management agencies, as well as with active citizens. The chapter considers how future developments might impact on key areas such as police legitimacy, structure, pluralisation and the police mission. The continued extension of police responsibilities, amidst a context of seemingly endless legislative reform since the mid-1990s, has created a lack of clarity about what the core role and function of the police is. Indeed, in 2005, Commissioner of the Metropolitan

Police Sir Ian Blair, called for an urgent review of policing and bemoaned the lack of serious public debate about the role of the Police Service in society. This chapter draws on more recent calls by Sir Hugh Orde, head of the Association of Chief Police Officers (ACPO), for the first fundamental review of policing since 1962 (BBC News, 2010) and discusses how this, or other reviews of policing, might influence future policy developments as well as other issues discussed in previous chapters of the book.

The proposed Liberal–Conservative police reforms that emerged during 2010 seem to provide significant continuities with the community orientation evident in previous Labour policy and the evolution of the police role over the last two decades. From a police perspective, rather than constituting a break with the past the reforms point towards a renewed emphasis on integrated approaches to crime reduction through partnership work and community engagement, a view that is supported by more in-depth analysis of the debate surrounding the Police Reform and Social Responsibility Bill (Home Office, 2010a,b). This chapter puts the current policy agenda in context by providing an overview of the twenty-first century policing landscape in the UK and the impact that this has had on the police role and policing processes more generally. Contemporary developments in policing will be explained using relevant criminological theories before the second half of the chapter concludes the book by introducing three hypothetical futures for policing. This final section encourages the reader to think about what sort of policing societies want and how this should be delivered.

REFLECTIVE TASK

This chapter looks at the broader impact of social, cultural and political changes upon policing structures and the police role and function. One way of monitoring the impact of these changes upon the police is by engaging with new policy initiatives and legislation and evaluating their effectiveness on police performance or public confidence in the police. In your opinion, which policing policies stand out as having been most successful? Why?

A review of the policing landscape

The current emphasis upon co-ordinated criminal justice responses to crime reduction is not new. The Crime and Disorder Act 1998 required the police to work in partnership with other statutory agencies, particularly local authorities. This partnership approach encouraged a view that crime fighting should no longer be the sole remit of the public police, a factor that was further emphasised in the Police Reform Act 2002. A multitude of crime and disorder partnerships subsequently emerged across the country to address the problem of crime through multi-agency initiatives that addressed specific problems within communities. At the same time, the increasingly significant role played by private security agencies since the Second World War was finally acknowledged, and to some degree validated, by the Private

Security Industry Act 2001. The private security sector provides protective and pre-ventive functions in areas as disparate as shopping centres, clubs and bars, private investigation and the development of CCTV systems. The Private Security Industry Act represented statutory acknowledgement of the role of commercial partners in the provision of policing services. Together, these legislative developments re-shaped and restructured the policing landscape.

This re-structuring of policing resulted from a recognition that the majority of police time and resources were spent providing assistance and reassurance to the public. This included perfunctory functions such as making the public feel safer through a uniformed presence on the street and the removal of signs of social dis-order. Home Office evidence had indicated that crime reduction targets alone were not improving public confidence (Innes et al., 2002) and that the police needed to provide a visible local presence and actively engage with communities to improve public confidence in community safety strategies. These reforms acknowledged the contribution the police had played in crime reduction since the mid-1990s but recognised that public trust in the police had simultaneously decreased and that fear of crime had continued to rise.

Blair's (2003) three-section altarpiece model of policing became a central part of the police response to the broader re-structuring of policing provision and the enhanced emphasis on public reassurance. The three sections cover:

- the traditional agenda of volume crime, public order and responding to emer-gency calls;

- serious (and organised) crime and terrorism;

- anti-social behaviour (and the need for reassurance policing).

Blair pointed towards the historical absence of focus on this third section of the altarpiece and a need to reform the police in response to public demand in this area. When Sir Ian Blair first became Commissioner of the Metropolitan Police in February 2005 he asserted the importance of section three for 'normal' people and advocated the introduction of uniformed PCSOs to increase the visibility of policing. This led to an increase in uniformed foot patrol through the establishment of PCSOs and other local authority figures with limited police powers. Blair's proposal led to PCSOs, police officers and volunteer special constables forming small neighbourhood units that worked in specific areas in order to improve relationships with local communi-ties. The shift towards neighbourhood policing since 2006, and as a national strat-egy since 2008, represented a further acknowledgement of the need to respond to public demand and enhance the order maintenance function of the police role.

PRACTICAL TASK

Have a look at Sir Ian Blair's 2003 speech on the future of policing (www.padpolice. com/futureofpolicing.php). How did Blair envisage the police role changing in the future?

In addition to enhancing public reassurance Sir Ian Blair also argued that police reform would re-assert the importance of police work as a 'public good' and avoid the privatisation of substantial components of the policing role. Blair argued that responding to public demand was an essential part of the police role in a consumer society and that this 'responsiveness' would stop the future privatisation of key aspects of the community policing role that had been witnessed in the US, South Africa and other countries (Jones and Newburn, 1998). A more detailed and vivid example of the problems created by the fragmentation and privatisation of policing is provided by Davis (1990) in his book *City of Quartz*. Davis's book examines social segregation in Los Angeles where the affluent neighbourhoods on the outskirts of the city are defended by secure gates and private security firms while the poor neighbourhoods in the urban centre are regulated through the use of curfews and a militarised police force.

Alongside concern about the fragmentation of policing provision at the community level, the combined threat of terrorism and the increasingly international nature of some crimes meant that international crime agencies, such as Interpol and Europol, have increasingly played a role in supporting state police agencies. Social, political and cultural changes at both the global and local levels have expanded the network of plural policing to meet the demands of societies that place crime and security among its foremost public concerns. Separating, and responding to the twin threats of terrorism/security and community safety/reassurance represents a significant challenge for policing in the UK and is a key driver behind police reform. To help provide some clarity here, Brodeur (1983) characterises this distinction as a separation between:

- 'High' Policing (trans-national policing of organised crime and terrorism) and

- 'Low' Policing (the struggle for sovereignty and community safety at local levels).

In order to meet the challenges set out here, policing has evolved and in place of the monolithic model of the traditional thin blue line we now have an increasingly diverse network of security provision. This was acknowledged by the head of Her Majesty's Inspectorate of Constabulary (HMIC), Flanagan (2005) in his assessment of the reorganisation of the Police Service when he referred to the broad need of providing 'protective services' in addition to traditional policing.

PRACTICAL TASK

Have a look at this 2010 BBC article about Sir Hugh Orde's call for a review of policing (http://news.bbc.co.uk/1/hi/uk/8579663.stm). According to this article, why does Orde think that the structure of the Police Service needs reviewing?

A review of the police role and function

As previous chapters have highlighted the core function of the police role is often presented as a balance between crime fighting and peace-keeping (or order maintenance). Criminologists have focused on the role of the police as peace-keepers and supported this argument with countless empirical studies. Pioneering criminologists such as Banton (1964) and Skolnick (1966) demonstrated that the police play a key role in keeping the peace and that this is achieved through the deterrent value of the Police Service's uniformed presence on the streets and the coercive threat of their legal power to use force (Bittner, 1980). This debate about the role and function of the police, when placed in a political and economic context that aims to influence the future of policing, becomes a discussion about the best use of finite police resources.

Studies in the US and the UK have frequently shown that no more than 25 per cent of calls made to the police concern crime directly and, at times, this figure has dropped to between 15 per cent and 20 per cent (Bayley, 1994). This is because a phone call that reports a crime may turn out to be inaccurate or may be the responsibility of another agency. Thus, crime is a relatively minor part of everyday patrol work (Morris and Heal, 1981). Even if a report to the police about a crime is accurate by the time they arrive the offender is often long gone. This undermines the traditional view of day-to-day police work being primarily concerned with crime fighting and raises questions about the use of highly trained police officers in the management of minor misdemeanours. As Banton (1964, page 85) acknowledged many years ago, *waiting, boredom and paperwork* are core parts of the police role, yet this mundane side of the role is displaced in police organisational culture, media-driven imagery and the public psyche by a focus upon the dramatic and the extraordinary.

The 1996 Audit Commission report, 'Streetwise: Effective Foot Patrol', indicated that 75 per cent of police resources were taken up with front-line roles. This includes patrolling by foot or car and criminal investigation. The reactive and resource-intensive nature of policing arises because the public are the most significant determinants of what the police actually do on a day-to-day basis. The public make the 999 calls that determine how police officers are deployed. In cities, over 90 per cent of patrol work is generated by calls to emergency numbers (Bayley, 1994). Because of this, the police's mandate is much wider than crime and frequently strays into public nuisance, anti-social behaviour and other broader social issues. Patrolling is the most resource-intensive task that the police perform. In England and Wales, 56 per cent of officers perform patrolling functions. After patrolling, the next largest use of resources for the police is criminal investigation, which accounts for around 15 per cent of police personnel. The third biggest area involves the regulation of traffic, which accounts for 7 per cent of police officers in England and Wales, although this had rapidly decreased due to the growth in number of speed cameras and the development of the Highways Agency. The rest of police time is predominantly taken up with administrative work which accounts for approximately 7 per cent of police officers in England and Wales (Bayley, 1994).

Therefore, it is clear that the majority of police time is spent providing assistance and reassurance to the public. It is this background knowledge that led Sir Ian Blair to call for a renewed emphasis on reassurance policing, making the public feel safer through a uniformed presence on the street and the removal of abandoned cars, shopping trolleys, graffiti and street-level drug dealing, an acknowledgement of the important psychological function of 'signal crimes' (Innes et al., 2002). This represented a re-articulation of Wilson and Kelling's (1982) Broken Windows thesis that had influenced Police Chief Bill Bratton and Mayor Giuliani in New York in the middle of the 1990s. Blair cited the successful role the police in the UK had played in helping to decrease crime since the mid-1990s, as measured by official crime statistics and the British Crime Survey; yet he also acknowledged that the public's trust in the police had diminished. The police needed to re-engage with their traditional role, demonstrate that they had a visible local presence and respond more directly to the concerns of individual communities in order to improve public confidence in community safety strategies (Tuffin et al., 2006). This perspective was provided further support by an HMIC report (2010, page 3) that stated that only 11 per cent of total police resources were visible and available to the public at a given time. Thus, police reform remains an ongoing concern on the current government's agenda.

These reforms present an ongoing challenge to the traditional police role alongside the threat of the further pluralisation of policing service provision. The multiple functions of the post-modern, community-orientated police and their partner agencies seem here to stay. More recently the Home Office called for the better use of police volunteers. The Home Office (2010a,b, page 84) acknowledged that there were already 29,000 volunteer magistrates; 6,500 volunteers in Victim Support; 15,000 special constables; 6,000 police support volunteers; and over 3.1 million Neighbourhood Watch members but that the role of the volunteer should be extended to incorporate even more policing functions. The available empirical evidence demonstrates that the public associate a strong police presence with the absence of crime (HMIC, 2010), thus providing continued support for growth in the use of volunteers to plug the reassurance gap that Sir Ian Blair and others had identified.

PRACTICAL TASK

The HMIC report (2010), Valuing the Police: Policing in an Age of Austerity (www.hmic.gov.uk/sitecollectiondocuments/Value%20for%20Money/VTP_NFS_20100720.pdf), sets out a challenge for police forces to perform their central role and function while also introducing financial cuts of 25 per cent between 2011 and 2014. Have a look at the report and try to answer the following questions.

- *What does the HMIC report identify as being the core role and function of the Police Service?*

- *How will police forces be able to continue to provide a high quality service to the public during a period when their funding is due to be cut?*

The police and policing

The continued re-structuring of the Police Service, coupled with the broader re-shaping of policing, requires us to think about policing and security in new ways. As the contemporary policing agents of sovereign governments struggle to maintain a sense of control over 'problem neighbourhoods' and 'crime hotspots' within a climate of heightened uncertainty regarding the threat of international terrorism and trans-national organised crime, state resources have become stretched. As the earlier part of the chapter outlined, this has led to a growing number of agencies becoming involved in policing and the provision of security (Jones and Newburn, 1998; Button, 2002). In the private security industry, a small number of trans-national commercial organisations, such as Group 4 Securicor and Securitas (see their websites, www.G4S.com and www.securitas.com, for more information) have benefited from a climate within which central governments are increasingly sub-contracting the provision of security to the commercial sector. Traditional policing functions such as prisoner transfer, roads policing and custody management have been sub-contracted to commercial organisations while technological developments such as Airwave, automatic number plate recognition (ANPR) and forensic services have been developed by, or via, the commercial sector.

Post-modern policing agencies increasingly concentrate upon the identification of risks, targeting offenders as aggregates rather than individuals, before assessing the means of their control and management utilising the most cost-effective measures (Feeley and Simon, 1992). Within this context it becomes possible to think about how the responsibility for regulating the spatial distribution of individuals across time and space is, in certain circumstances, being sub-contracted to the commercial sector that subsequently takes on this outsourced, sovereign function. This requires us to continually question which policing functions have to remain with the Police Service and which can be contracted-out without generating enhanced security threats and undermining public legitimacy.

Following on from this, there has been a burgeoning of theoretical discourse about 'policing' and 'security' among criminologists, understood sometimes as a public good and, at other times, as a commodity that can be bought and sold (Johnston and Shearing, 2003; Zedner, 2004; Stenson, 2005). A central theme in this discourse has been the claim that the state (as far as we are concerned, 'the Police Service') has a diminishing role to play and that there has been a pluralisation of 'security' providers, which is re-shaping the structure of policing across the globe. This makes it possible, or even encourages us to envisage, the increased marketisation of security, a future that Davis has warned us against. The market model of security as a mode of governance claims that growth in commercial security is a response to increasing demand for protection in the face of increasing uncertainty, threat and hazard, which cannot be met by the state police (Johnston and Shearing, 2003; Jones and Newburn, 2002). Hence, from this perspective, security is no longer seen principally as the function of the sovereign nation-state and traditional large public sector institutions no longer maintain a privileged position in providing security; they are understood simply as one node of security among others in the commercial, voluntary and statutory sectors (Johnston and Shearing, 2003).

In this instance, technologies of population management, which address mobility across borders, trans-national crimes and the threat of terrorism, become a different way of conceptualising security. As a consequence of this, rival policing agencies from different sectors are involved in shifting alliances with the state and a plethora of other agencies, or interest groups, with the aim of furthering their own interests and values, in alignment with and alongside sovereign law and state institutions. From this perspective, the state generates the market space for new organisations to enter the policing arena from the statutory, voluntary and commercial sectors through new policies and legislation. The struggle for sovereign power involves a wide range of different groups attempting to assert their own agendas by aligning them with the interests of the state and sovereign law. Although the law provides authority and legitimacy for the ideas and interests of those in power, the exercise of sovereign power itself remains contested and this encourages criminologists to think about what the future of policing may look like. The above example highlights how politics and culture play a key role within the exercise of sovereignty and the maintenance of security. Current UK policy envisages a greater role for the voluntary sector in policing, yet if this gap is not filled by voluntary groups then the space may be seized upon by commercial agencies with new policing services for sale. This re-thinking of policing and security allows us to imagine three distinct possible futures for policing.

The future shape of policing

The Coalition government's communitarian focus on enhancing informal social controls and communal bonds helps us to foresee a future landscape of policing in which conscientious citizens play an active role in policing social order. This represents a further shift in thinking about the policing of societies that re-interprets the role of the Police Service from being monopoly providers to being just one service provider among a multitude of others from the statutory, voluntary and commercial sectors. Furthermore, in many ways, this represents an ideological shift back in thinking to pre-modern (or neo-feudal) societies in which systems of informal social control dominated at the local level prior to the establishment of a professional police. This shift in discourse about the police and policing encourages us to think about what the potential future shape of policing will look like. Gordon Hughes (1998) has identified three possible futures for crime control in societies that are experiencing this shift to active citizenship at the same time as an increase in demand for policing resources among an anxious and uncertain populace. The following section uses Hughes' crime control vision as a model for the future of policing. The section adapts and updates Hughes' three futures to situate them in their twenty-first century policing context. The three categories are as follows.

- The active community.

- The active community and authoritarian policing.

- Exclusionary policing.

The active community

This is the policing future that is currently being advocated by the UK government in the Police Reform and Social Responsibility Bill (Home Office, 2010a,b; although its exact manifestation is yet to become clear) and which involves a multitude of different community partnerships that work alongside the Police Service. The active community emphasises the democratic potential of partnership approaches, particularly in terms of building pressure to address crime problems through radical political, social and economic strategies that empower citizens and encourage their involvement in policing. This perspective views the processes of globalisation as generating a renewed focus on local community engagement and the creation of *civic and inclusive safe cities* (Hughes, 1998, page 146). The police's role in this process is evident in recent Home Office (2010a,b, page 12) policy documentation that highlights their role in 'Integrated Offender Management'. This approach sees a range of partners including police, probation, prisons, local authorities, and voluntary partners working together to tackle the offenders who cause most harm in their communities'.

The Liberal–Conservative coalition has ring-fenced funding for PCSOs for the next two years, proposed further expansion of the volunteer special constabulary and enhanced community consultation, all policies that emerged under the previous administration. Thus, the ongoing re-structuring and re-branding of the Police Service as a local, community-orientated and engaged service is exemplified by the police embrace of restorative justice philosophies and localised political reform, as exemplified in the establishment of police and crime commissioners. As is the case elsewhere in the criminal justice system, the twin drivers here are a desire to increase community confidence in the police coupled with an acknowledgement of the state's limited capacity to manage problems of crime and disorder by itself (or to afford to pay for them!).

The political emphasis placed upon the importance of 'community' in public policy coupled with the Third Way focus on moral authoritarianism and communitarian values has helped to promote the profile of bottom-up, active community strategies such as restorative policing and local political representation. Most clearly, distinct commonalities exist within contemporary political discourse in the fields of both restorative justice and policing surrounding active citizen participation, social inclusion, community cohesion and improved informal social controls that aim to foster more civilised, self regulating conduct among citizens. This policy focus attempts to improve police legitimacy through the enhancement of democratic structures that re-build Durkheim's mechanical solidarity (or high levels of informal social control) within post-modern communities where this is perceived to have broken down. The extent to which this re-construction of (big) society is possible remains a moot point and has been discussed throughout this book.

An active community is an essential constituent of successful policing in the Liberal–Conservative vision of the Big Society. Have a read through Innes's (2010) article on policing in the Big Society (www.upsi.org.uk/storage/Innes%20-%20 Policing%20Big%20Society%20PR121110.pdf) and then have a think about the following questions.

- *Which types of policing strategies could be provided by an active community?*

- *How well do you think these policing strategies will work?*

The active community supported by authoritarian policing

Although much has been made of the re-structuring of policing in this chapter it is important to not overstate the extent to which the role of the public police has diminished. The Police Service remains distinct from other policing providers because of their legal powers to use coercive force. In affluent democracies with a large public sector like the UK this ensures that the Police Service has retained a central cultural and symbolic function in the maintenance of social order that separates them from policing agencies from the voluntary and commercial sectors. Both Beck (1992) and Giddens (1990) argue that late modern society is character-ised by risk, an absence of trust and ontological insecurity. This presents a challenge to the idea of a Big Society of active citizens as it points to the detachment of indi-viduals from their community and the breakdown of social ties. Therefore, instead of an active community with strong informal social controls, post-modernists such as Beck and Giddens help us to imagine a potential future where communities are supported by a strong authoritarian state. From this perspective, the collective val-ues of the Big Society are reinforced by authoritarian policing that aims to restore order in fractured communities where the informal social controls and traditional social ties that are central to the active community are missing.

Instead of the active community we have *high trust authoritarian communitarian societies* (Hughes, 1998): strong moral communities supported by a strong authoritar-ian state. This perspective is tied theoretically to Wilson and Kelling's (1982) Broken Windows thesis as it foresees the police retaining a central and symbolic role in the maintenance of social order, much as they have done for the past 200 years, but in support of a multitude of other policing providers. From this perspective, the police act as a symbolic authoritarian body that re-asserts the hierarchical and disciplinary nature of society; enforcing social norms where they are perceived to have broken down. Furthermore, the police become key players in neo-conservative moralising whereby individuals and groups deemed to be at-risk are targeted by high-profile policing strat-egies supported by extensive media coverage and 'populist punitive' messages from state officials that aim to re-build a sense of security among the wider citizenry.

Within the hyper-reality of late modernity, images of policing carry a symbolic value that dominates public discourse about policing. Public debate about the role of policing in society is generally surrounded by poor-quality information, misinterpretation and media-driven hyperbole about threats to order. This provides the police with an important symbolic role and function coupled with a mystification that surrounds their day-to-day practice (Reiner, 2010). Part of the reason for the absence of sustained debate about the police role, as bemoaned by Sir Ian Blair and Sir Hugh Orde, is due to the emotive context that the debate about policing takes place within. To understand this, Garland (1990, page 8) encourages us to look beyond policing agencies and the offenders they seek to control to understand contemporary debates about the role and function of the police and policing. Instead, it is important to look at *the onlookers, whose sentiments are first outraged and then re-assured*. This type of analysis focuses upon individual and collective responses to policing and is closely linked to the Durkheimian perspective on crime, and criminal justice responses to it, as an 'expressive', or emotive, institution. This perspective helps us to understand the importance of reassurance policing and fear of crime within contemporary societies. As Garland (1990, page 4) concludes, crime control *is a cultural as well as a strategic affair; it is a realm for the expression of social value and emotion as well as a process for asserting control*.

REFLECTIVE TASK

Identify as many sources of information about crime and policing as you can. How do these sources portray the problem of crime, policing, and the effectiveness of the latter in combating the former?

Exclusionary policing

Davis's (1990) *City of Quartz* remains the most vivid exposition of the threat of exclusionary developments in policing and crime control. Davis's depiction of crime control in Los Angeles revolves around the militarisation of urban policing in a *fortress city*, characterised by *privatism and social exclusion* (Hughes, 1998, page 138). In the fortress city, those who have wealth have the power to use exclusionary techniques against 'others' as they create safe and secure private enclaves in suburban areas that are policed by private security personnel. This removes financial support for community policing strategies and encourages urban policing strategies that focus on the management and containment of risks using militarised forms of policing.

Aspects of Davis's Los Angeles have become part of the architecture of crime control in the UK. The exponential growth of CCTV in the UK throughout the 1990s and its function creep into congestion charging, speed cameras and ANPR embodies Davis's fear of urban areas becoming characterised by their security strategies, which focus upon those deemed to be most at risk. In this exclusionary model, private modes of policing have become dominant, security has become commodified, and the wealthy purchase security while the poor are left exposed to the consequences of crime and disorder. Davis's Marxist perspective foresees future cities being characterised by a comprehensive architecture of policing and security that is embodied in security patrols, omnipresent surveillance and carceral urban design for the poor and the 'other' while the rich are socially segregated and live in secure gated communities.

In a society that is experiencing a rapid growth in the amount of repressive hardware available for the governance of its citizens it becomes increasingly important to defend the need for equal justice and to understand the mechanisms that drive growth in policing, particularly in the private security industry. The growth of policing surveillance technologies, such as ANPR, a multitude of inter-connected databases monitoring personal data and mobility, and even airborne drones that were originally designed for use on foreign battlefields, target specific 'at-risk' populations in attempts to regulate and govern conduct while also managing public and private space through the exclusion of unwanted groups. It is clear that unregulated growth in commercial policing presents a potential threat of inequitable policing provision and, more generally, the over-policing of society, yet, the attraction of commercial policing for financially constrained governments remains clear. By outsourcing or contracting-out services to the commercial sector central government is able to expand the crime control system, and thus meet the political demand for enhancing security, while also deviating around economic and fiscal restraints (Singh, 2005).

PRACTICAL TASK

Have a look at this news article (www.bbc.co.uk/news/uk-10888985). Is this an example of exclusionary policing or a necessary response to threats to security and order?

Marxist perspectives on policing often have a dystopian edge to them. Have a read through the following short article for an introduction to a more subtle example of exclusionary policing (www.popcenter.org/problems/crimes_against_tourists/PDFs/Shearing_Stenning_1997.pdf).

Criminological futures

Having introduced three potential policing futures (and there are many more) for you to review and evaluate, the final section of this chapter asks you to identify where you think the police should fit into policing and what you think their role and function in society should be.

As the first chapter in this book outlined, the role of criminological study of the police has historically been separated into three distinct categories.

• Sociological analysis of the police and policing.

• Cultural analysis of the police institution.

• Critiques of the police role and function, philosophies and strategies.

Analysis of the changing landscape of policing, the evolving role and function of the public police and the identification of the future shape of policing points us towards a very different future for the criminological study of the police and policing. The criminological sub-discipline of police studies fits neatly in to the first two of the three prospective futures outlined in this chapter. In the first example, police studies provides a framework for analysing the public role of the police and their position as a formal state institution surrounded by a multitude of community policing providers and active citizens. In the second example, police studies provides a means of evaluating the effectiveness of the state police in maintaining order, providing reassurance and controlling crime. Here, the emphasis of police studies is very much on the implementation of policy and the professional role of the Police Service.

The third example is much more broadly concerned with the development of a fragmented structure of policing in which the public police no longer perform a central role. This example requires us to extend our focus beyond traditional police studies and to engage in the more critical criminological and sociological scholarship of the police and policing. The sociological study of policing retains a broader focus on policing as a social process which aims to maintain order unlike the more administrative approach of police studies, which retains a narrower focus on evidence-based policing strategies, problem-solving and policy evaluation. Critical perspectives on policing question the structural foundations of policing as much as their role in society and are subsequently concerned with questions surrounding police governance and legitimacy ahead of the efficacy of different policing strategies. Post-modern developments in policing scholarship will ensure that different criminological schools of thought flourish in the future and continue to embrace the divergent consensus and conflict perspectives on the role of policing that have been introduced in this book. This provides a further opportunity to reflect on your own thinking about the police and policing.

CASE STUDY

It is time to go back to Everytown, which we first visited in the introductory chapter. Everytown had received an increased amount of coverage in the local and regional media about its crime and disorder problems. Everytown is an area of mixed tenure properties with predominantly local authority tenants where residents have been complaining about groups of anti-social young people, drug misuse and dealers operating from flats and phone boxes. There had also been an increase in concern about the amount of criminal damage and graffiti. Stories about low-level offences have been reported in the local newspaper on a regular basis and this had led to a rise in fear of crime among Everytown's residents. As Everytown's new policing and community safety officer, you have been tasked with designing a response to these problems on behalf of the local residents.

- *What sort of policing response is needed to manage the problems that the area is facing?*

- *How, if at all, has your answer to the question above changed since you first read the introductory chapter of the book?*

C H A P T E R   S U M M A R Y

Competing narratives about community orientation, national security and public accountability make it increasingly difficult to answer the question – what is the role and the function of the police? An ever-changing policing landscape coupled with tension between policing, security and order maintenance at the local, national and international levels has made it more difficult to police a more demanding British public and simultaneously address the global nature of twenty-first century threats to security and order. Recent attempts to promote greater citizen participation in policing are just one component of broader attempts to re-assert the central role of the community in policing; yet, at times, this ideological shift runs contrary to the historic policing mission where independent police professional knowledge directs local developments. This presents a clear challenge to the shifting sands of the police role and the drift to community-orientated policing. Within British policing, police culture has long been characterised by an anti-centralist, strongly localist tradition where police leaders maintain a high degree of control over local policing policy. In addition to this, the focus on performance indicators that has dominated policing for the last decade has led to a cultural focus on incident management and resolution ahead of long-term problem-oriented strategies. These are the some of the challenges that face the Police Service at the beginning of the twenty-first century. The authors do not claim to provide definitive answers to these manifold challenges but hope that they have provided an interesting introduction to some of the more important criminological questions that surround the ever-changing role of the police and policing in society.

FURTHER READING

The three policing futures outlined in this chapter have been adapted from Gordon Hughes' (1998) final chapter in *Understanding Crime Prevention*. A more policy-focused piece on this subject can be found on the US' National Institute of Justice website in Bayley and Shearing's (2001) *The New Structure of Policing*. The Home Office's website (www.homeoffice.gov.uk/police/) will keep you up to date with current policy developments in policing although this should always be supplemented with engagement with the multitude of academic texts and policing journals that are available.

REFERENCES

Audit Commission (1996) *Streetwise: Effective Foot Patrol*. London: HMSO.

Banton, M (1964) *The Policeman in the Community*. London: Tavistock.

Bayley, D (1994) *Police for the Future*. Oxford: Oxford University Press.

Bayley, D and Shearing, C (2001) *The New Structure of Policing: Description, Conceptualization and Research Agenda*. Washington: National Institute of Justice. Available online at www.ncjrs.org/pdffiles1/nij/187083.pdf (Accessed 20 December 2010).

BBC News (2010) Sir Hugh Orde Calls for Review of Policing. *BBC News, 22nd March 2010*. Available online at www.news.bbc.co.uk/1/hi/uk/8579663.stm (Accessed 28 January 2011).

Beck, U (1992) *Risk Society*. London: Sage.

Bittner, E (1980) *The Functions of the Police in Modern Society*. Washington D.C.: National Institute of Justice.

Blair, I (2003) Leading towards the Future. In *Future of Policing Conference*, 10 October 2003. Available online at www.padpolice.com/futureofpolicing.php (Accessed 27 January 2011).

Brodeur, J P (1983) High Policing and Low Policing: Remarks About the Policing of Political Activities. *Social Problems*, **30**(5): 507–20.

Button, M (2002) *Private Policing*. Cullompton: Willan.

Davis, M (1990) *City of Quartz*. New York: Vintage.

Feeley, M and Simon, J (1992) The New Penology: Notes on the Emerging Strategy of Corrections and Its Implications. *Criminology*, **30**(4): 449–74.

Flanagan, R (2005) *Final Report of the Independent Review of Policing*. London: HMIC.

Garland, D (1990) Frameworks of Inquiry in the Sociology of Punishment. *British Journal of Sociology*, **14**(1): 1–15.

Giddens, A (1990) *The Consequences of Modernity*. Cambridge: Polity.

Her Majesty's Inspectorate of Constabulary (2010) *Valuing the Police: Policing in an Age of Austerity*. London: HMIC.

Home Office (2010a) *Police Reform and Social Responsibility Bill*. Cm 116. London: Stationary Office.

Home Office (2010b) *Breaking the Cycle: Effective Punishment, Rehabilitation and Sentencing of Offenders*. Cm 7972. London: Stationary Office.

Hughes, G (1998) *Understanding Crime Prevention*. Maidenhead: Open University Press.

Innes, M (2010) What Impact Will the Government's 'Big Society' have on Policing? Universities Police Sciences Institute. Available online at www.upsi.org.uk/storage/Innes%20 % 20Policing%20Big%20Society%20PR121110.pdf (Accessed 31 January 2011).

Innes, M, Fielding, N and Langan, S (2002) *Signal Crimes and Control Signals: Towards an Evidence Based Framework for Reassurance Policing*. Guildford: University of Surrey.

Johnston, L and Shearing, C (2003) *Governing Security*. London: Routledge.

Jones, T and Newburn, T (1998) *Private Security and Public Policing*. Oxford: Clarendon.

Jones, T and Newburn, T (2002) The Transformation of Policing? Understanding Current Trends in Policing Systems. *British Journal of Criminology*, **42**(1): 129–46.

Morris, P and Heal, K (1981) *Crime Control and the Police: A Review of Research*. Home Office Research Study No. 67. London: HMSO.

Reiner, R (2010) *The Politics of the Police*, 4th edition. Oxford: Oxford University Press.

Singh, A M (2005) Private Security and Crime Control. *Theoretical Criminology*, **9**(2): 153–74.

Skolnick, J (1966) *Justice Without Trial: Law Enforcement in a Democratic Society*. New York: Wiley.

Stenson, K (2005) Sovereignty, Biopolitics and the Local Government of Crime in Britain. *Theoretical Criminology*, **9**(3): 265–87.

Tuffin, R, Morris, J and Poole, A (2006) *An Evaluation of the Impact of the National Reassurance Policing Programme*. Research Study 296. London: Home Office.

Wilson, J Q and Kelling, G (1982) Broken Windows. *The Atlantic Monthly*, **249**(3): 29–38.

Zedner, L (2004) *Criminal Justice*, Oxford: Oxford University Press.

Index